The Fundamentals of Trade Finance

3rd Edition

JOSEPH F. GRECO, PH.D
& BRIAN MURRAY

Distribution by Bublish, Inc.

ISBN: 978-1-64704-286-8 (Paperback)
ISBN: 978-1-64704-288-2 (eBook)

CONTENTS

PART 1

Trade Today

CHAPTER 1

Introduction to Trade

Growth and Direction of Trade

The business world is becoming increasingly globalized. Evidence of this can be seen in the growth of the World Trade Organization (WTO) exists to promote free and fair trade around the globe. In addition, the North American Free Trade Agreement (NAFTA) as well as the European Union (EU), the two largest trade blocs, have also been factors in the expansion. All three were conceived and established in the last half century. Added to these factors, technology and economic integration will continue to foster the growth of trade into the future. With these new opportunities, small businesses can now engage in importing and exporting more now than any time in history.

Exporting

When exporting, there are two different approaches small businesses can take: direct and indirect. Each method will entail different responsibilities for the business or a third party. Businesses wishing to engage in exporting can either take a hands-on approach (direct) or allow others to manage the risk (indirect).

Direct Exporting occurs between an exporter and importer, with no third party involved. The business can appoint either an agent or a distributor to assist in the process. An agent finds a buyer for the products in other countries but is paid a commission as agents do not take title to the goods. On the other hand, a distributor will purchase the goods, take title to them, and resell them to importers in the target country. **Indirect Exporting** is typically done by businesses that are new to exporting. An intermediary such as an export management company (EMC) will assume the risks and costs of international trade for its clients, the exporter. With general knowledge of the product and foreign markets global traders can service manufacturers who do not otherwise export. This service is important since many new exporters may not have the knowledge or capacity to engage in international business.

Importing

Whether it is a small wholesaler or a large multinational corporation, **importing** is the export process reversed. Most importers purchase foreign products to sell for a profit in the domestic market. Importing can result in lower consumer prices by increasing domestic price competition. Other nations may have the advantage of lower labor costs as well as skilled workforces. U.S. companies can capitalize on this advantage and import products to sell at more competitive prices.

Top 5 Countries Exported Year-to-Date, December 2018	Dollar Amount Exported (Billions)
Canada	288.7
Mexico	265.0
China	120.3
Japan	75.0
United Kingdom	66.2

U.S. Trade Opportunities

Information about the United States exports and imports can be found on the United States Census Bureau which offers not only year-to-date information from each month of the year but also monthly information on the top trading partners. Additionally, they offer trade highlights of each year and month. So for 2018 there were more imports than exports. In fact, $3.121 billion was imported and $2.5 billion was exported which accounts for a $621 billion deficit. During the recession, the goods and services deficit was $708.7 billion. Some of the U.S.'s other top trading partners are also experiencing a higher than normal deficit. In 2018 most of the top trading partners have a deficit with the exception of the United Kingdom. Since they do not manufacture many goods and it is expensive to import goods from EU the UK must heavily import goods from the United States. In fact, the United States is the top trading partner for the UK for both exports and imports but the UK is only a top trading partner for the US in terms of exports.

Top 5 Countries Imported Year-to-Date, December 2018	Dollar Amount Imported (Billions)
China	539.5
Mexico	346.5
Canada	318.5
Japan	142.6
Germany	125.9

In 2018, China sold more than twice the amount of exports to U.S. than the U.S. sold to China ($539.5 billion). Canada and Mexico remain the top trading partners because of NAFTA. This allows the United States, Canada, and Mexico to trade with each other without the harsh restrictions, duties, or tariffs placed on agriculture, manufacturing, and services. Additionally, it allows smaller businesses to do more operations with Canada and Mexico because it would be less expensive. NAFTA has created a strong bond between the three countries who will most likely remain top trading partners.

Setting up the Business

One of the first steps in creating a business is choosing how it will be legally organized. The correct form depends on the situation, so it is important to know what structure is right for your purposes. All businesses must choose from sole proprietorships, partnerships, and corporations such as a private C-Corporation or a limited liability company (LLC). Each have their advantages as well as disadvantages. To make a wise decision, a business owner must first anticipate projected revenues, start-up costs, tax structure, and liabilities.

Sole Proprietorships

The simplest form of business to organize, a **sole proprietorship** (SP) does business where one person has the liability and oversees all the decisions.

Sole proprietorships have certain advantages, that include:

1. They are easy to start and dissolve. Very few legal documents and licenses are required, unlike the case with corporations.
2. SP's are taxed at the individual federal and state business rates. Depending on the net income produced by the company, the tax rate may be an advantage for a smaller business.

While these advantages exist, SP's offer little in the way of business knowledge, protection from liability and easy access to capital. The proprietor is limited to relying on their own field of limited expertise while personally unlimited in their liabilities from the business. Any legal suits directed at the business become a personal burden. Funding is limited to the owner's wealth and income which many times limits working capital. Another disadvantage is that SP's terminate on the death of the owner.

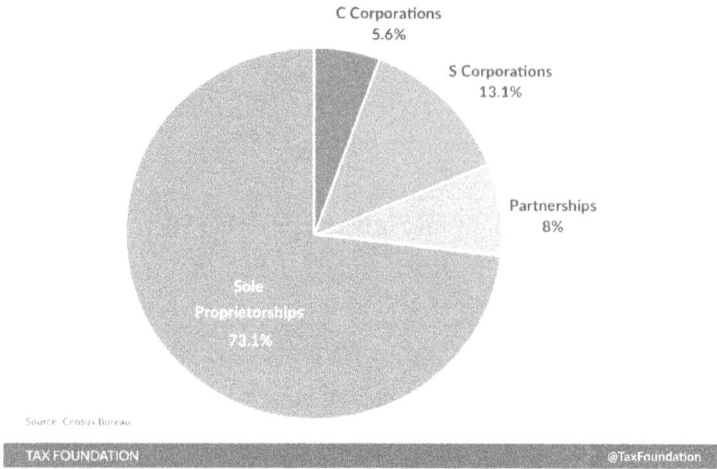

C Corporations
5.6%

S Corporations
13.1%

Partnerships
8%

Sole
Proprietorships
73.1%

Source: Census Bureau

TAX FOUNDATION   @TaxFoundation

Figure 1.1 Sole Proprietorships are a majority of all business

Pomerleau, Kyle. "An Overview of Pass-through Businesses in the United States." *Tax Foundation,* 9 Feb. 2017, taxfoundation.org/overview-pass-through-businesses-united-states/. Figures from United States Census Bureau

Partnerships

Partnerships are like SP's, but the main difference lies in the sharing of responsibilities and profits between two or more owners. There are no legal formation documents, but it is typical for partners to have an attorney draft a partnership agreement. The agreement should outline the rights, responsibilities and exit plan of each partner. Partners fall into one of two categories: general or limited partners. A general partner assumes unlimited liability for actively managing the business. A limited partner must play no active managing role and can only lose what they originally invested.

Unlike SP's, partnerships can capitalize on the skills of each of the partners, making for a stronger organization. With multiple partners, the amount of their assets can improve their ability to finance the business. Partner profits are considered personal income and taxed similar to an SP. The death or withdrawal of an owner from the agreement results in the termination of a partnership. Finally, with more people involved in the decision making comes a higher probability of conflict. It is no surprise that partnerships have the highest failure rate.

Corporations

Corporations are legal entities licensed by governments that can engage in all functions of a business. Being a separate legal entity from their owners, corporations can enter contracts and lawsuits and taxed at a corporate tax rate as opposed to a personal one. To form a corporation, a fee and application must be submitted to the secretary of state where the business is located. When approved, the government grants a certificate known as the articles of incorporation. This document authorizes the issuing of stock.

Two ownership structures exist for corporations: public and private. A public corporation issues stock available for purchase on public stock exchanges, with anyone able to buy and sell shares and receive part of the profits in the form of dividends. Private corporations issue stock, but it is not traded on a public exchange.

The main advantage to a corporate structure pertains to liability. Being a separate entity means the corporation's assets and liabilities are separated from the owner's personal assets. This separation is known as the corporate veil. Corporations continue to operate even if a key stockholder dies. In this case, ownership passes to the next of kin. Therefore, corporations have unlimited life as long as government fees continue to be paid. Despite these advantages, incorporating a business requires much more time and expense. Since they must be formed through the state or federal government, the amount of fees can vary greatly. Federal and state governments may subject corporations to more stringent legal and financial reporting requirements. Since corporate profits are separated from personal income, they are subject to corporate federal, state and local taxes.

Ownership & Accounting Differences	
C Corporation	**S Corporation**
• More tax-free status on fringe benefits	• Less tax-free benefits for shareholders
• Can have multiple classes of stock	• Limited to one class of stock
• Can choose when fiscal year ends	• Fiscal year must end December 31st
• Bigger corps. required to use accrual accounting method	• Only those with inventory have to use accrual accounting method

Figure 1.2 C-Corporations vs. S-Corporations

"The Differences Between an C Corporation Vs. an S Corporation." *PayTech*, 7 Feb. 2020, pay-tech.com/differences-arizona-c-corporation-vs-arizona-s-corporation/.

S-Corporations and Limited Liability Companies

S-Corporations are considered pass-through entities. All profits that the corporation receives passes directly through its shareholders. This also passes the tax liability to the shareholders and the corporation does not pay corporate taxes. Owners of S-Corporations are subject to marginal tax rates just as individual wage earners. The degree of involvement an owner has in the S-Corporation determines how much the owner pays in taxes. Owners are required to pay federal, state, and local income taxes. Although wages are taxed, profit distribution is not. Because of this, S-Corporations pay very little in wages and instead distribute a significant amount in profit instead.

S-Corps can be formed under the following conditions:

1. The business is incorporated domestically (Within the U.S.) Unaffiliated with another organization
2. No more than 100 shareholders
3. One class of stock
4. Shareholders must be individuals or estates that reside within the U.S
5. Passive investment must be less than 20% of corporation's income

Many small businesses will find it easy to qualify for this treatment. Unlike SPs and partnerships, S-Corps are not subject to self-employment taxes. The IRS requires that all shareholders pay taxes in proportion to their equity.

As the name would suggest, a **Limited Liability Company** (LLC) limits the personal liability of shareholders. LLC's pay no federal income tax. Shareholders instead pay tax on their share of the profits. While an LLC is very similar to an S-Corp, it offers much more flexibility. Members can decide how to divide profits and losses. Unlike S-Corps, there is no limit to the number of partners or restrictions on where they are from.

Business Checking Accounts

Since 2001, new bank rules have made it more challenging to open a business checking account. All businesses, regardless of their function, must have a checking account to make payments. When engaging in trade, an international bank will have specialized processes for foreign payments, such as letters of credit and factoring. With an international network, these banks may also be a resource for finding overseas contacts and doing due diligence on your foreign partners

The following documents required by banks to open a business checking account depend on the legal structure of the business.

Sole Proprietorships

1. Social Security Number or Federal Employment Identification Number (FEIN)
2. Business License showing both business and owner's name, or
3. Business name filing document, such as a Fictitious Name Certificate, also known as a Doing Business As (DBA), showing both business and owner's name

Partnerships

1. FEIN
2. Partnership Agreement showing business name and name of partners, and
3. Business name filing document, such as Fictitious Name Certificate or DBA, showing business name and name of partners

Corporations

1. FEIN
2. Articles of Incorporation or Certificate of Incorporation
3. Corporate Resolution identifying authorized signers if officer names are not listed on Articles of Incorporation or Certificate of Incorporation
4. Business name filing document, such as Fictitious Name Certificate or DBA, showing business name and name of partners

Limited Liability Companies

1. FEIN
2. Articles of Organization or Certificate of Formation
3. Corporate Resolution identifying authorized signers if officer names are not listed on Articles of Organization or Certificate of Formation
4. Business name filing document, such as Fictitious Name Certificate or DBA, showing business name and name of partners

References

Business Formation: Choosing a Structure. (n.d.). Retrieved from https://www.legalzoom.com/business/business-formation/inc-overview.html.

Open a business bank account. (2018, September 9). Retrieved from https://www.sba.gov/business-guide/launch-your-business/open-business-bank-account.

Starting a Business. (n.d.). Retrieved from https://www.irs.gov/businesses/small-businesses-self-employed/starting-a-business.

CHAPTER 2

International Trade Agreements

Barriers to Free Trade

Trade barriers are government regulations placed on international trade. Most economists agree they are detrimental and decrease economic efficiency. Trade barriers work on the general principle: imposing restrictions that reduce the flow of a traded product. The downside of trade barriers occurs when two or more nations repeatedly use trade barriers against each other, leading to a trade war. Barriers take two forms: tariff and non-tariff. Tariffs include fees that are placed on mostly exports from a country. Non-tariff barriers include subsidies, embargoes, quotas and exchange controls. As governments regulate trade, they have the authority to create restrictions on international transactions in the following ways:

Tariffs

A tariff is a tax on imports or exports by a nation's government. It may have several motives. Traditionally, tariffs have been used as a source of government income. They also may be used to encourage or safeguard domestic industries.

All U.S. imports are subject to duty or duty-free entry, which depends upon their classification in the tariff schedule. For products that are subject to duty, three different methods are used to collect tariffs.

1. Ad valorem tariff: the tariff collected is a percentage of the value of the import product.
2. Specific tariff: The tariff rate is based on the physical unit or weight of the import because the same rate is applied to all goods in this category tend to be more restrictive on low-priced goods.
3. Compound tariff: Compound tariffs combine both ad valorem and specific tariffs. An example would be a fee or $1.50/lb and 5% ad valorem.

Subsidies

A subsidy is a sum of money granted by the government as a form of support to a specific economic sector. The purpose is to increase sales and, in the process, promote the government's intended economic policy. Subsidies may come in various forms. An export subsidy supports products that are exported in order to balance a nation's exports versus their imports.

Import Quotas

An import quota is a trade restriction that sets a physical limit on the quantity of imports allowed into a country in a given time period. The purpose of the quota is to reduce the competition for import-competing domestic goods and to benefit its domestic producers in the domestic economy

Embargoes

An embargo is a government order restricting all exporting to and importing from a foreign nation. The purpose of an embargo is commonly political. For example, one country protests the actions of another, so its government decides to stop all trade. The ultimate purpose is to negatively impact the offending economy and force its government to halt the offensive actions. For example, U.S. exporters and importers are embargoed from trading with Iran, North Korea and Cuba.

Exchange Controls

Exchange controls are government restrictions on foreign exchange transactions. The purpose of exchange controls is to limit the amount of a specific currency leaving the country and to prevent a nation's unfavorable balance of payments. In order to achieve this, businesses are often required to call any foreign exchange coming into their possession to government-designated authority, which is usually the central bank

Foreign Capital Controls

Foreign capital controls are measures generally used to restrict access by a nation's citizens to foreign assets. In this case, the control as a capital outflow control. For example, China imposes a strict limit on the amount of currency per person that leaves the country. On the other hand, when foreigners are restricted from investing into a country, the controls are known as a capital inflow control. Since developing countries are most vulnerable to volatile capital reserves, foreign capital controls are generally stricter in these countries than in developed countries.

Regional Economic Integration

Economic integration is a process to increase between countries. Its aim is to reduce tariffs for both producers and consumers. The long run goal is to remove barriers to foreign trade so that members can share a common market and consistent fiscal policies. Regional economic integration is important for natural resource management, especially in extractive industries. It makes an important contribution to a country's economic growth when it is combined with the broader economy of other countries. The advantages of economic integration are that it promotes global advantages for businesses. It allows countries to unify and form common markets that create larger markets by opening borders and eliminating tariffs between member nations. The five levels of economic integration include the following: a free trade agreement, a customs union, a common market, an economic union, and a political union.

Free Trade Agreement (FTA)

In free trade agreements, barriers such as tariffs and quotas are removed between members, but each member sets its own policy for nonmembers. An example of a free trade agreement would be the North American Free Trade Agreement (NAFTA) that exists between the United States, Canada, and Mexico. Under NAFTA, tariffs or quotas have been reduced or eliminated between the three countries.

Customs Union

A customs union is a trading agreement that is composed of a bloc of countries member to a free trade agreement with common external tariffs. The purpose for establishing a customs union is to increase economic efficiency and to establish closer political and cultural ties between member countries. Some examples of customs unions include the Andean Community (CAN), the Caribbean Community (CARICOM), the East African Community (EAC) and the Southern African Customs Union (SACU), to name a few.

Common Market

A common market is a group of countries who impose few or no duties on trade with one another but a common external tariff on trade with other countries. In addition to this, a customs union allows for free movement of money and workers among member states. For example, the European Union is a common market that has a common 10% tariff on cars imported into it.

Economic Union

An economic union is a common market that involves more than one nation based on a mutual agreement between member countries to permit the free movement of financial capital, workers, and goods/services. Many economic unions require the coordination of social, fiscal, and monetary policies among participating nations. When an economic union involves unifying its currency, it becomes a monetary union.

The European Union (EU) is probably the most commonly cited example of an economic union. The member countries coordinate the economic policies, laws and regulations so that they can work together to address economic and financial issues. The EU also has a common currency, the Euro, used by 19 of its 28 members. This is known as the European Monetary Union (EMU).

Political Union

A political union is a form of economic integration that combines members into a single state. Unlike an economic union, members of a political union share a central government and the union is recognized internationally as a single country. The most common examples of political unions include the United States, Canada, and India.

The World Trade Organization (WTO)

Following the Second World War, a proposal was made for an institution to promote and regulate international free trade. A provisional agreement known as **The General Agreement on Trade and Tariffs** (GATT) was established during these negotiations. The GATT specified general obligations that all the signatories were required to observe.

Establishment of the WTO

The Uruguay Rounds took place between 1986 and 1994 after a U.S. proposal to broaden the scope of GATT. Aside from tariff reduction, GATT needed to cover specific services, intellectual property and investment. By liberalizing trade, the negotiations would also help bring developing nations into new international markets. Tariffs were reduced by 40% across the board and new rules were put in place to prevent unfair trade practices such as subsidies and dumping.

Members of the WTO can pursue regional agreements with each other given that certain conditions are met. The WTO rules require that a 10-year plan for creating free trade on most goods and refrain from raising tariffs on nonmembers of the agreement. The amount of regional agreements has steadily increased since the WTO's founding in 1995.

195 agreements have been proposed since 1995, with 112 in effect. Most of these agreements (~80%) are bilateral intended only for easier market access and do not require extensive coordination between participants. Less than ten percent propose harmonization, which is the creation of identical standards within the market.

Most Favored Nation Status

When the WTO grants a most favored nation status, all parties must treat one another in the same way with respect to duties and tariffs. Imports are treated the same way as domestic products. Some exceptions do exist. For example, member states of NAFTA or the EU are exempt from treating all other countries with such favor as they are already practicing this on a smaller scale. Under the most favored nation status, a member country is not allowed to discriminate between trade partners. If a special status is granted to one trade partner, it is required to extend that same status to all members of the WTO.

Liberalization

Liberalization policies were intended to facilitate trade between the participating countries. GATT provided a forum for negotiations that reduced barriers to trade. Trade ministers met regularly at periodic conferences (known as "rounds"). The Uruguay Rounds beginning in 1986 led to eventual establishment of the WTO in 1995. Since 2001, the Doha Rounds have been taking place with the goal of creating a more favorable trade environment for developing countries.

Trade Disputes

A member country that believes it has been harmed because another member country has violated GATT rules can request arbitration.

Member countries are permitted to protect their own producers from unfairly priced imports. If trade occurs outside of GATT regulations, retaliatory measures may be approved in the form of duties or tariffs to offset the damage. As such, GATT mitigates the potential for trade wars.

The Agreements on Trade Related Aspects of Intellectual Property Rights (TRIPS) narrowed the gaps in the way intellectual property rights are protected around the world by bringing them under common WTO rules. All members of the WTO must comply with existing and future GATT standards. Any violations of these standards could be brought to the WTO for review, complete with resolutions and appeals procedures.

European Union

The European Union (EU) is an economic integration of 28 member states located primarily in Western and Central Europe. With a population of 508 million in an area of 1.67 million square miles, it was founded on November 1st, 1993 with headquarters in Brussels, Belgium. Since 1993, the EU has grown from the six founding states of Belgium, France, Germany, Italy, Luxembourg and the Netherlands to the current 28. To become a member of the Union, member nations subject themselves to privileges and obligations. Some of these criteria require a stable democracy with respect for human rights and the rule of law, a functioning market economy, and the acceptance of EU laws.

Dating back to the Treaty of Rome in 1957, the concept of an economically integrated Europe is nothing new. After the Second World War, it was important to create peace on the continent through trade. Countries that trade with one another are unlikely to go to war. Being made up of so many small countries, unification allowed the advantages of economies of scale to compete in a global market.

Member States

Austria, Belgium, Bulgaria, Croatia, Cyprus, Czech Republic, Denmark, Estonia, Finland, France, Germany, Greece, Hungary, Ireland, Italy, Latvia, Lithuania, Luxembourg, Malta, Netherlands, Poland, Portugal, Romania, Slovakia, Slovenia, Spain, Sweden, United Kingdom (Brexit)

28 FLAG EUROPEAN UNION COUNTRIES

AUSTRIA BELGIUM BULGARIA CROATIA CYPRUS CZECH DENMARK

ESTONIA FINLAND FRANCE GERMANY GREECE HUNGARY IRELAND

ITALY LATVIA LITHUANIA LUXEMBOURG MALTA NETHERLAND POLAND

PORTUGAL ROMANIA SLOVAKIA SLOVENIA SPAIN SWEDEN UK

Figure 2.1 EU Member States

Stock Photo Courtesy of Freepik.com

Institutions of the EU

In the EU's institutional setup, the EU's broad priorities are set by the European Council (EC). In the European Parliament, directly elected members represent the European citizens. The interests of the EU as a whole are promoted by the European Commission. The European Court of Justice ensures that EU law is interpreted and applied the same in every member country.

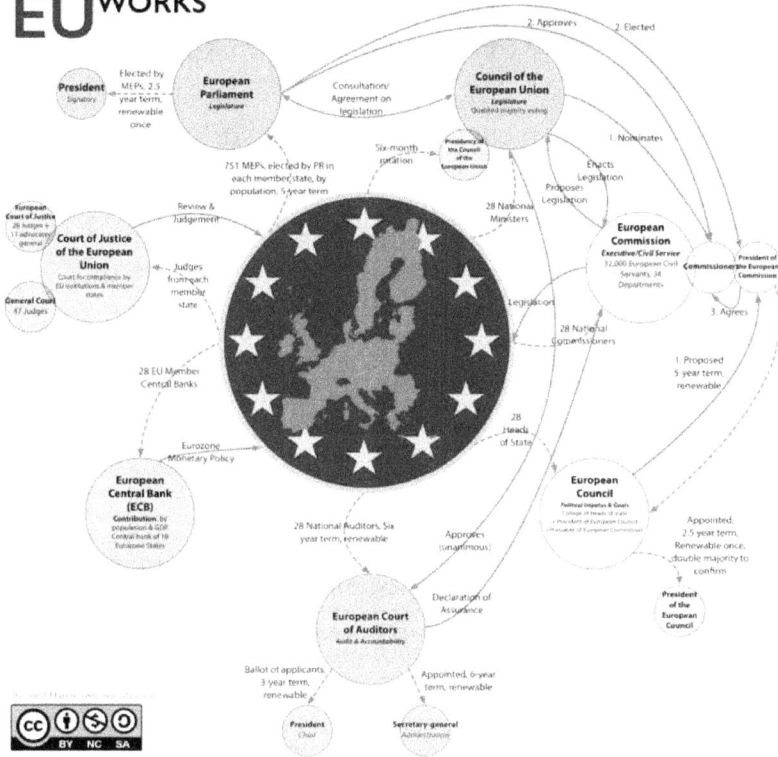

Figure 2.2 Institutions of the EU

Harris, Richard. "Democratic Clarity." *Two Worlds: Intelligent Reality*, 6 Mar. 2020, two-worlds.com/democratic-clarity/.

The European Council

The role of the EC is to define the general political direction and priorities of the European Union. The members are composed of the heads of state of the EU countries and the EC president. It is not one of the EU's legislating institutions. Rather than negotiating or adopting EU laws, the Council sets the EU's policy agenda by adopting conclusions during meetings which identify concerns and actions to be taken. The council passes laws, approves budget proposals, develops foreign policy, and co-ordinates anti- crime strategies.

The EU Parliament

The role of the directly-elected parliament includes legislative, supervisory, and budgetary responsibilities. The EU has given parliament a broad range of powers. Together, with representatives of the EU's governments in the council, parliament is responsible for adopting EU legislation under the ordinary legislative procedure, both the parliament and the council equal co-legislators. There are currently sitting in are 751 elected members from all the member states combined.

The European Commission

The European Commission promotes the general interest of the EU by proposing and enforcing legislation as well as implementing policies and the EU budget. Every five years, 20 commissioners are appointed by each member state. Large nations appoint two while smaller nations appoint one. The Commission proposes legislation, implements EU policies, law enforcement, international coordination and describes how political priorities will be turned into concrete actions. The Commission's work program sets out a plan of action for the next 12 months.

The European Court of Justice

The role of the Court is to ensure EU law is interpreted and applied the same in every EU country. The members of the court include 11 advocates general. The court constitutes the judicial authority of the European Union. Member states appoint judges every six years. These judges are tasked with settling disputes arising from the treaty

EU Regulations

The 1957 Treaty of Rome outlined the goals of an integrated Europe:

- Promote free trade among members, as well as a common external tariff on non-members
- End all restrictions on the free movement of labor, services, and capital between member states. All members must give the national treatment standard to other member countries
- Create a unified transportation, agricultural, and competition policy

Over time, most of these objectives were accomplished. The Common Agricultural Policy of 1962 set common prices for agricultural products that stabilized income for farmers. All members eliminated tariffs between one another and established a common external tariff by 1968. Nonetheless, removing the nontariff barriers proved a difficult and slow process.

To facilitate the integration process, the EC proposed the Single European Market Act. In 1986 the objectives of this proposal were as follows:

- Create a common market by removing all physical and technical barriers to trade between member states. This was achieved by removing customs controls at borders and harmonizing taxes to aid competition and transparency.
- Shift towards a common currency through monetary cooperation. The Maastricht Treaty of 1992 eventually led to the adoption of the euro currency.
- Standardize working conditions across the community of member
- Cooperate on research, development and an environmental policy

North American Free Trade Agreement

The United States had been a driving force in promoting free trade after WWII. This was demonstrated by their efforts in creating the GATT/WTO. Due to the size of the multilateral agreements, the inefficiency of large-scale negotiations became apparent. As such, regional agreements became the favored alternative. Following the suit of the EU, the U.S. worked with its neighbors and closest trading partners, Canada and Mexico. The resulted in NAFTA that gradually eliminated tariffs on most goods traded between its members, creating a free trade area in North America. Second in population only to the European Union, the combined GDP of the pact exceeds $25 trillion as of 2018. As of 2019, the United States/Mexico/Canada Agreement (USMCA) as a replacement for NAFTA. Approval is currently pending on the legislatures of the participating countries.

Benefits to NAFTA Member Countries

Canadian businesses can achieve economies of scale by operating larger plants. NAFTA opens a larger consumer market for Canadian exports.

The USMCA benefits the three countries in the following ways:

- Automobiles: A key component of the agreement involves automobiles. For Canada to qualify for zero tariffs, 75% of a car's parts must be made in the three countries. In addition, 30% of a manufacturing of car needs to be completed by workers who earn at least $16 per hour, moving up to 40% by 2023. This change is a win for both the American and Canadian auto sectors as it moves more manufacturing moves away from Mexico. It also would likely reduce the amount of an automobile that can be made using parts from China, Malaysia, or Vietnam. The agreement also includes a provision prohibiting the U.S. from imposing a tariff on Canadian auto imports.
- Dairy: According the new agreement, Canada must open its milk market to the United States. This change, a big win for U.S. dairy farmers in Wisconsin and New York, gives the U.S. access to a

new market of Canadian ultra-filtered milk processors. Despite protectionist inclinations in the United States, these uncertainties can be addressed by NAFTA's dispute resolution.

- Labor: The Agreement requires Mexico to improve the collective bargaining capabilities of its organized labor. It requires Mexico to comply with the International Labor organizations convention 98 on freedom of association and collective bargaining. Other measures include a minimum wage for the automobile industry. This measure will be phased in during the first 5 years after the treaty's ratification.

- Intellectual Property (IP): The agreement extends the copyright length in Canada to life plus 70 years and for recordings 75 years. It also extends the patent for biologics such as vaccines to 10 years. This improved the existing standard in Canada from eight years and Mexico from five years.

- Currency: A new addition to the agreement includes macro-economic policies and exchange rate matters. This is considered important because it sets a precedent for future trade agreements. The agreement establishes transparency requirements for currency trading, which, if violated, constitute grounds for a dispute appeal. The three countries are all currently in agreement with these transparency requirements.

- Dispute Settlement: The USMCA continues the three dispute settlement mechanisms included in NAFTA that is Chapters 11 , 19 and 20. Chapter 11, known as investor-state dispute settlement (ISDS), enables multinational corporations to sue participating governments over allegedly discriminatory policies. Considered the most controversial of the settlement mechanisms, the Canadian negotiators gave Canada full exemption from ISDS three years after NAFTA has been terminated. Chapter 19 specifies that USMCA panel hears disputed cases and acts as an International Trade Court in arbitrating the dispute. Chapter

20 is the country-to-country resolution mechanism and regarded as the least contentious of the mechanisms carried over in the original NAFTA. Disputed cases would involve complaints between USMCA member states that a term of the agreement had been violated.

Before NAFTA, the U.S. was in a free trade agreement with Canada. NAFTA allowed this relationship to continue and expand. By including Mexico in the agreement, America could influence Latin American nations away from state-controlled markets. The U.S. receives over 80% of exports from Canada and Mexico, while being the largest investor in both countries.

NAFTA provides access for Mexican goods and services in the U.S./Canadian market. Lower labor costs encourage foreign direct investment in Mexico while creating more well-paying jobs. This growth would help return capital flight, create less incentive for illegal immigration and provide a new market for American exports.

NAFTA Regulations

NAFTA members incorporated the GATT rule of "**most favored nation**" when trading with one another. This rule states that countries cannot discriminate against similar imported goods. Aside from tariffs, NAFTA's aims were to reduce customs fees, export taxes and licensing requirements. For these goods to be given such preferential treatment, their production must originate within the NAFTA region. Regarding services, each party cannot treat any banking, insurance, telecommunications and transportation services less favorably than their own.

The Association of Southeast Asian Nations (ASEAN)

Regional integration is not unique to Europe and North America. While Asia is not nearly as integrated as the rest of the world, there are cooperation efforts to reduce poverty by boosting economic growth through trade. The region contains a high level of economic diversity. Major international players include Japan, South Korea, Taiwan, Hong Kong, and Singapore. Emerging economies include China, India, Vietnam and the Philippines. Southeast Asia is also home to the less-developed countries of Laos, Cambodia, Nepal, Bangladesh, and Myanmar.

While most agreements in Asia are bilateral, there are notable exceptions, such as the **Association of Southeast Asian Nations** (ASEAN). Made up of Vietnam, Thailand, Cambodia, Singapore, Myanmar, Malaysia, Laos, Indonesia, Brunei and The Philippines, it is the world's largest economic agreement by population. ASEAN was formed to build a community comprised of three pillars: Political Security, Economic Cooperation and Socio-Cultural cooperation. While the goal of tariff reduction has been on an accelerated timetable, there has been slower progress on removing non-tariff barriers.

The ASEAN community pursues it goals to improve the lives in the region through economic and cultural development, social progress, regional peace and security/collaboration, mutual training assistance and research, improvement of living standards, and cooperation with regional and international organizations. It offers new opportunities to the region and the world for a new atmosphere of peace and stability, of more open and rules-based markets for business, of better health and education and of sustainable development. Due to the amount of trade that passes through the region, maritime security is important. With ASEAN, Southeast Asia will continue to promote stability and economic growth.

References

STAS, M. (2019, October 29). Easy to read–The European Union. Retrieved from https://europa.eu/european-union/about-eu/easy-to-read_en.

McBride, J., & Sergie, M. A. (2018, October 1). NAFTA's Economic Impact. Retrieved from https://www.cfr.org/backgrounder/naftas-economic-impact.

World Trade Organization–Global trade. (n.d.). Retrieved from http://www.wto.org/.

CHAPTER 3

Political Risk

B usinesses that engage in international trade face a wide variety of risks that can negatively affect day-to-day operations. These risks range from nonpayment, lost cargo, foreign currency depreciation, to unstable political situations. Political risk stems from the governments' decisions or events that occur in the importing country and can take the form of a variety of events. These include armed conflicts may result in the destruction or confiscation of cargo. Foreign governments can impose strict bureaucratic barriers in the form of quotas, currency controls, and licensing. These risks are most likely to be faced when working in developing economies.

Risk Management

To monitor political situations in foreign countries, private firms and governments agencies offer insights in the form of published materials on potential risks in the short to medium term. Published reports can be acquired through government agencies, such as the Export/Import (EXIM) Bank and the Commercial Service housed in the U.S. Dept of Commerce. The Commercial Service provides Country Commercial Guides for every country the U.S. trades with. The Commercial Guide includes sections on Doing Business in the country, the Political and Economic Environment, Selling U.S. Products and services, the Leading Sectors for U.S. Exports, Trade Regulations, Trade Financing, and Business Travel. The EXIM bank also offers a wide variety of programs to insure U.S. exporters. Private providers include the Political Risk Services (PRS Group Inc.), the Economist Intelligence Unit (EIU), Euromoney, and the Business International Corporation.

Culture: A Form of Risk

Culture, as it relates to international business, is the human-made part of the environment. Some refer to it as a society's design for living. Market behavior relates directly to the culture, since markets constantly adjust to cultural demands. Cross-cultural cooperation can provide diversity of knowledge and approaches to business but can also result in conflict if not handled carefully. The lack of cross-cultural cooperation can threaten the success of any global transaction. What might be a common business practice in the U.S. may not be acceptable and even offensive to other cultures. To be sensitive to other cultures is a key to international success, as business customs are a product of the culture. Culture mainly effects the business transaction in the areas of communication and organization.

Context

Context describes the circumstances that form the setting for the transaction. High-context cultures place a great deal of emphasis on the circumstances that form a transaction. These cultures are more dependent on group consensus and rely more on implicit and nonverbal communication. Without understanding the culture's background, it can be difficult to understand messages sent by the other side. African, Asian, Middle Eastern and Latin American countries are examples of high-context cultures. In these cultures, one's identity is tied to the group. Relationships are built slowly and require a high level of trust. Tone, facial expressions and gestures are significant indicators and verbal messages are more indirect than to the point. Disagreement by the other side may be taken personally, so high-context individuals can be more sensitive to conflict. For example, in Chinese culture expressing a negative opinion may be considered poor social behavior.

Low-context cultures value individualism, privacy and explicit communication. Less implicit and nonverbal communication is required to convey a message. The United States, Australia, and other cultures with roots in Western Europe are considered low-context cultures. For example, a US exporter will move directly to the issue of pricing faster than an importer from a high-context culture. This directness may often be misunderstood as unwanted behavior by the high-context cultures. One's identity is based on their perception of themselves and their accomplishments. Low-context relationships are formed easily but may end quickly. Nonverbal cues are not significant to communication, and verbal messages are direct and to the point. Disagreement is detached from the individual and focus is on creating rational solutions. Criticisms are not to be taken personally but meant to be constructive with the goal of problem-solving.

Timing: Monochronic vs. Polychronic

When dealing with cross-cultural communication, time needs to be effectively managed in order to complete projects. The perception of time varies greatly across different cultures. This can create conflict and delays when working internationally. Projects can involve different cultural groups and estimates of time may not be accurate. Differing cultural attitudes towards time can make negotiating and problem-solving less efficient. Picture a scenario in the United Arab Emirates (UAE). An American exporter is looking to secure an important deal with a potential partner. They probably are on a tight time schedule and trying to avoid wasting time. Their counterpart in the UAE may constantly show up late to appointments. Interruptions are not uncommon, with phone calls and papers being signed in the middle of meetings. The American exporter begins to lose patience but could risk being offensive and losing the deal if they express frustration. To prevent conflict, it is important to understand how the concept of timing differs from monochronic and polychronic.

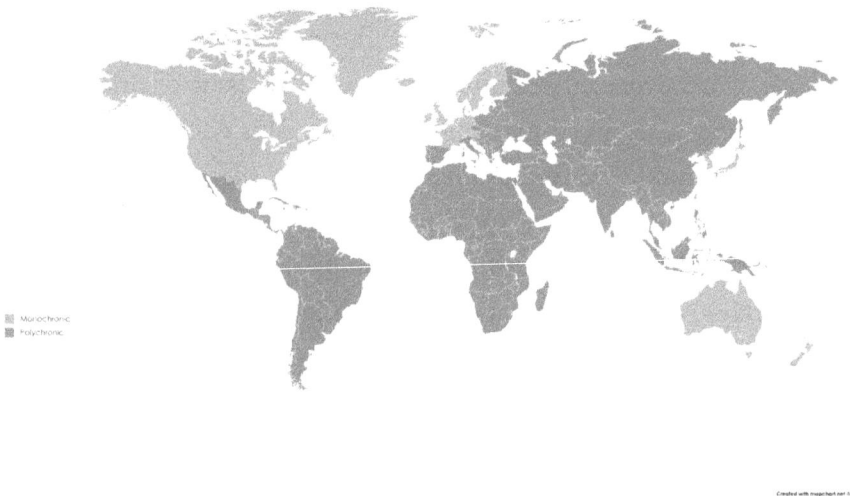

Figure 3.2 Map of Monochronic and Polychronic cultures (click to enlarge) Based on Morden, 1999; Kotabe and Helsen, 2001

Monochronic

As the name implies, monochronic cultures value punctuality and focus on one task at a time. Order is linear when it comes to timing. Time is a valuable commodity and schedules are strictly adhered to. The task at hand has priority and must be accomplished with as little interruptions as possible. Monochronic cultures tend to also be low-context. Efficiency is valued more than relationships and meetings are focused on the objectives rather than the people involved.

Polychronic

Polychronic cultures prefer to multitask. Meetings and phone calls may intersect, which may result in interruptions. These interruptions are managed by simply shifting the schedule. The emphasis is placed on the people involved in a task rather than the details of the task itself. Polychronic cultures tend to also be high context cultures. Personal relationships are valued over business deals, and timing is flexible in order to build them.

Business Norms

Aside from the communication and the perception of time, each culture will have its own set of rules known as business norms. The first impression given to a potential partner could make or break a deal. To avoid wasting time and money, it is important to understand the proper etiquette of conducting business.

Introductions

Each country will have its own way to physically greet somebody. This can range from handshakes, bows, or even a kiss on the cheek. An exchange of gifts is typically customary, but depending on the local custom, the gift should not be too expensive as it may make the recipient feel guilty. Most Asian cultures see the business card as an extension of oneself, so they must be offered with both hands to be taken seriously.

Americans may be on a first name basis with all their colleagues, reserving titles for only those in executive positions. Many cultures may consider this rude. When being introduced, a businessperson should listen closely to how they are introduced and reciprocating by addressing them in the same way. It is usually safe to use someone's title and last name until you are invited to do otherwise. Countries like Germany put a high value on titles, and those with advanced degrees expect to be recognized for their accomplishments, going so far as to even having three titles such as *Herr Professor Doktor* (Mister Professor Doctor).

Professional Attire

Another important part of etiquette involves appropriate clothing that must be worn to make a lasting impression. While an industry may allow for casual wear, it may or may not apply to the other company or country the businessperson is visiting. Some cultures forego the typical suit jackets but may pay attention to the quality of the clothing (e.g. custom-tailored suits). When in doubt, it is always best to dress conservatively with darker colors and few accessories.

Conversing

English is the primary language of international business, so if you are conducting business in a foreign country, it is likely that your counterparts speak it to some degree. Be sure to speak concisely and clearly as possible. Allow them to make mistakes and avoid the temptation to correct their speech. Be open to learning the language of your partners and demonstrate your appreciation of their culture. During conversations, avoid getting too personal with new acquaintances. Some cultures avoid talking about money, politics or religion, so go into meetings armed with acceptable topics such as the history or culture of your host country.

Customs

The success of global business can often be placed at risk when exporters and importers are unaware of the business customs surrounding their transactions. There are at least three levels of business customs: imperatives, adiaphora, and exclusives. These levels define the acceptable topics of conversation.

Imperatives

At the imperative level, exporters and importers are required to follow accepted rules of behavior. For example, an imperative business custom agenda times are strictly enforced and conversation is limited to the topic at hand.

Adiaphora

The adiaphora level means the exporter and importer have a choice of whether to adhere to certain behaviors. For example, a Japanese trader might bow upon greeting. Rather than bow, an American trader may choose to shake hands. Neither choice threatens the success of the transaction.

Exclusives

At the exclusive level, the exporter must adhere to the business norms of the importer's country. For example, it is generally accepted in the United States that discussion of political opinions and religious beliefs do not constitute a legitimate part of a business transaction. Such discussions are considered an exclusive right given in the U.S. to the American exporter and not the foreign importer. For a foreign trader to bring politics or religion into the conversation in the U.S. would threaten the life of the agreement.

References

Neese, B. |. (2019, January 31). Intercultural Communication: High and Low Context Cultures. Retrieved from https://online.seu.edu/articles/high-and-low-context-cultures

PART 2

Foreign Exchange

CHAPTER 4

Exchange Rates

The Foreign Exchange Markets

The global economy is now more interconnected than at any time in history. Changes in one region of the world are rapidly transmitted to those who are trading with the region. The changes are reflected almost simultaneously in the value of the nation's currency. Therefore, global traders continually face a loss of their nation's currency value (depreciation) or a gain (appreciation). In this chapter we will attempt to provide an understanding of one of the most misunderstood and largest financial markets in the world, the currency market. The foreign exchange or currency market where currencies are traded is not located in any one physical spot such as the New York Stock Exchange but is an electronically-linked network of currency traders, who may be bankers, brokers, and dealers. Their function is to bring together buyers and sellers of currency at various exchange rates.

What is an Exchange Rate?

An exchange rate is the price of one unit of foreign currency in terms a another. So, if you were to see the euro rate of exchange to the dollar is $1.20/€, it is a shorthand method that lets you know that the price of one euro in the U.S. would be $1.20. The euro is known as the reference currency to the dollar. On the other hand, the price of the dollar in France can be determined with the $1.20/€ rate. It is calculated as 1/$1.20 which yields the exchange rate in France with the dollar as the reference currency to the euro. In this example, the euro to dollar rate would be €.8333/$.

Exchange Rate Determination

The purpose of this section is to explain how exchange rates are set by the currency markets. In this section you will learn how exchange rates for foreign currencies can change the nature of an international transaction. First, we will look at how exchange rates come to be the spot rate. The spot rate is the exchange rate the last transaction completed and displayed currently. It represents the exchange rate that prevails worldwide at the present time. Be aware that this exchange rate may change in the next second. The major currencies in international trade are the following: the U.S. dollar, the European euro, the British pound, and the Japanese yen. At any time, the exchange rate for these currencies will change. The reason for this change is most often due to a change in the quantity demanded or the quantity supplied of the currency.

The Demand for Currency

Let us assume the following scenario: An American exporter purchases a German product such as a Mercedes-Benz car. There now exists in the currency markets a demand for the German currency, known as the euro.

Since the buyer of the German car must make payment in euros, he or she must go to the currency market to exchange their U.S. dollars for euros in order to complete this transaction. As we can see the demand for euros in the United States comes from the demand for German products by Americans. In this case the demand comes from the demand for the Mercedes-Benz car. The demand for euros is an inverse relationship between the possible exchange rate and the possible quantity demanded of the currency.

The Supply of Currency

When Americans demand German products, there must be a supply of euros to purchase to complete the transaction. The question now becomes "Where does the supply of euros come from in the U.S.?" The U.S. government does not print euros. Private companies in the U.S. do not print euros. Euros are printed by the EU Central Bank in Frankfurt. Then where does the supply in the United States of euros come from? The answer to this question is simple: the supply of euros comes from the demand by Germans for U.S. products. That means that when a German makes a purchase of an American good such as an iPhone, they must pay for it in U.S. dollars. To do this they must go to the currency market and sell their euros for US dollars. The effect of this transaction on the currency market in the U.S. is the creation of the supply of euros in the U.S. currency market. This means the supply of euros comes from the German demand for U.S. goods, in this case iPhones. Germans must convert euros to U.S. dollars to buy the imported phones. Whereas the demand for currency is an inverse relationship, the supply of the euros in the U.S. is a direct relationship between the exchange rate and the quantity supplied.

The Equilibrium Exchange Rate

The **equilibrium exchange rate** is the exchange rate where the quantity supplied of euros equals the quantity demanded of euros at a certain exchange rate. We say this is the equilibrium exchange rate, also known as the spot rate, because at this point there is no pressure on the exchange rate to increase or to decrease. What causes the exchange rate equilibrium to change?

How Exchange Rates Change

What causes exchange rates to change? Let's assume that there is an increase in demand by Americans for German cars. As more Mercedes cars are demanded, more euros are demanded at each possible exchange rate. Now there are several reasons why the demand would increase for the Mercedes cars. The simplest reason one can give that would cause a demand to increase at every possible exchange rate would be that Americans suddenly had more income to buy these cars. When the demand for the Mercedes increases at every possible exchange rate, it causes an increase in the demand for euros. What results is a new equilibrium exchange rate that is greater than the original rate. For example, when the original exchange rate is a $1.10/euro with the new demand, the exchange rate may rise to $1.15/euro.

Factors Affecting Exchange Rates

The supply and demand for the world's currencies changes constantly, and as the change so do the equilibrium exchange rates. Some of the factors that will cause these changes are inflation, interest rates, growth in a nation's Gross Domestic Product (GDP) and expectations of future exchange rates

Inflation

Inflation is most often defined as an increase in prices relative to other prices. In terms of global trade, when prices in the U.S. increase, leaving importers in the U.S. with less purchasing power. They are less likely to buy as many goods and services. They will be more likely to substitute where they can with locally produced goods and services. This leads to a decrease in the supply of euros at every possible exchange rate. They will be more likely to substitute where they can with locally sold goods and services leading to a decrease in the amount of euros supplied at every possible exchange rate. The result of the U.S. price change is a shift to the left of the supply for U.S. exports by EU residents.

Gross Domestic Product

A nation with strong economic growth will usually have a change in their gross domestic product each year that exceeds 3%. This strong growth will attract investment capital from abroad that seeks to acquire domestic assets. The increased demand for domestic assets results in an increased demand for the domestic currency, making it a stronger appreciating currency. On the other hand, nations with poor GDP growth will witness the exodus of investment capital and weaker, depreciating currencies.

The Forward Market

In addition to the spot market, there exists a separate market for currency. A forward contract, sold in the forward market between a bank and a hedger calls for delivery, at a fixed future date, of a specified amount of one currency against another. The forward exchange rate is fixed at the time the contract is executed. Although forward contracts exist for the most widely traded currencies, forward markets for the currencies of less developed countries are limited or nonexistent.

Case Study: Hedging with a forward contract

In a typical forward transaction, for example, a British exporter and a U.S. importer might negotiate a transaction that sells £100,000 of machinery in an invoice to the U.S. importer. Let's assume the transaction is based on 90 days of open account financing. On day one, we assume the spot rate is equal to $1.50/£. The first question the U.S. importer faces would if that exchange rate is available on day 89. Most likely, the answer will be no.

Importer's Choices

Choice #1

Day 1: U.S. Importer has three choices: 1. Do nothing until day 89 and then call the currency broker to buy £100,000 to pay the British exporter on day 90 at the current exchange rate for day 89.

What will the exchange rate be on day 89?

As stated earlier, the spot exchange rate will probably not be available on day 89, so the importer faces the possibility the exchange rate moves against them. In this case, the exchange rate to increase to more than $1.50/£ would cause a loss as compared to the spot of $1.50/£. At $1.50/£, the cost of the £100,000 invoice would be $150,000. If the spot rate on day 89 increases to $1.60/£ , the cost of £100,000 is $160,000, an increase of $10,000. How can the U.S. importer avoid this loss?

Choice #2

Rather than wait for day 89 to buy pounds to pay the British invoice, the U.S. importer could buy $100,000 pounds on day one at the current spot rate, deposit the pounds in a British bank account until day 90, and then pay the British exporter.

Problems with Choice #2

- It ties up the importer's cash (working capital) for the next 89 days, restricting the importer's ability to generate new business.
- There is no guarantee the exchange rate will maintain its value at the spot rate purchased on day one.
- The expense and time it will take may be extensive when finding a British bank and opening an account from a foreign country.

Choice #3

In choice #3, the importer calls their bank on day 1 and buys a forward contract that includes the following:

- £100,000 (a fixed amount)
- To be delivered on day 89 (at a fixed time)
- At an agreed upon 90-day forward exchange rate (a fixed exchange rate)

Let us assume that the forward rate is $1.55/£. In addition, the bank will charge a fee for the contract.

What is the best choice for the importer?

With the assumption that the dollar will depreciate over the 90-day period, so on day 90 the future spot rate is $1.65/£. Choice #1 is not the optimal choice since it will cost $165,000 to buy £100,000. Compared to choice #3, choice #2 still ties up the importer's working capital and costs the prevailing exchange rate on day 1. Choice #3 is the best. Why?

It costs $155,000 to purchase £100,000. If we assume the U.S. dollar continues to depreciate and the future spot rate on day 90 is $1.80/£, the importer has saved the difference between $180,000 (£100,000 x $1.80) minus $155,000. This would be a savings of $25,000 that the importer does not have to pay.

References

Bank for International Settlements. (n.d.). Retrieved from https://www.bis.org/.

Banton, Caroline. "How Are International Exchange Rates Set?" *Investopedia*, Investopedia, 12 Sept. 2020, www.investopedia.com/ask/answers/forex/how-forex-exchange-rates-set.asp.

Board of Governors of the Federal Reserve System. (n.d.). Retrieved from https://www.federalreserve.gov/.

FEDERAL RESERVE BANK of NEW YORK–Serving the Second District and the Nation–FEDERAL RESERVE BANK of NEW YORK. (n.d.). Retrieved from http://www.ny.frb.org/.

Mitchell, Cory. "How to Calculate an Exchange Rate." *Investopedia*, Investopedia, 28 Aug. 2020, www.investopedia.com/articles/forex/090314/how-calculate-exchange-rate.asp.

Part 3

The International Trade Transaction

CHAPTER 5

The Transaction

The Basic Transaction Model

The international trade transaction can be challenging for new exporters to traverse. A successful exporter needs to be familiar with negotiating terms, pricing methods and documentation. The final agreement between an exporter and importer specifies the price, quality, quantity, delivery, payment, inspections, packaging and insurance.

The Basic Transaction Model is as follows:

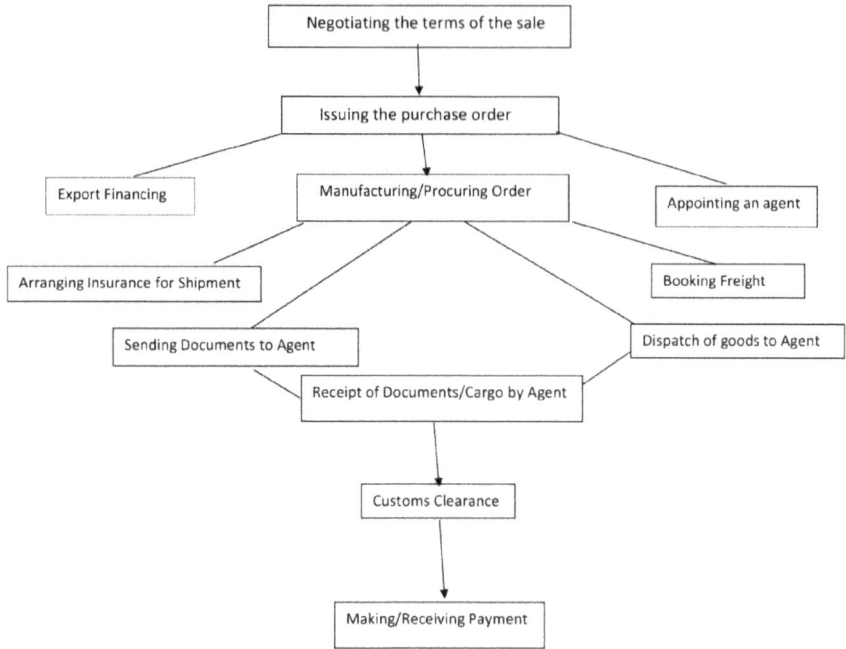

```
                    ┌─────────────────────────────────┐
                    │  Negotiating the terms of the sale │
                    └─────────────────────────────────┘
                                    │
                    ┌─────────────────────────────┐
                    │   Issuing the purchase order  │
                    └─────────────────────────────┘

┌──────────────────┐   ┌─────────────────────────────┐   ┌──────────────────┐
│ Export Financing │   │  Manufacturing/Procuring Order │   │ Appointing an agent│
└──────────────────┘   └─────────────────────────────┘   └──────────────────┘

┌─────────────────────────────┐                    ┌──────────────────┐
│ Arranging Insurance for Shipment │                 │  Booking Freight │
└─────────────────────────────┘                    └──────────────────┘

   ┌──────────────────────────┐           ┌──────────────────────────┐
   │ Sending Documents to Agent │          │ Dispatch of goods to Agent │
   └──────────────────────────┘           └──────────────────────────┘

          ┌─────────────────────────────────┐
          │ Receipt of Documents/Cargo by Agent │
          └─────────────────────────────────┘
                          │
              ┌──────────────────────┐
              │   Customs Clearance   │
              └──────────────────────┘
                          │
           ┌──────────────────────────┐
           │ Making/Receiving Payment  │
           └──────────────────────────┘
```

Figure 5.1 The Export Transaction Model

Negotiating the Terms of the Sale

Incoterms

Trade occurs between hundreds of countries, each with their own set of laws. When dealing with the import and export of goods, there are international standards in trade practices pertaining to the terms of the sale. The International Commercial Terms, commonly abbreviated as Incoterms, define the responsibilities of each party in the transaction. The responsibilities include but are not limited to the manufacture, labelling, and shipping of the goods. Depending on the terms followed, the exporter must factor in their obligations towards their costs. For example, a seller quoting EXW will charge a much lower price than CIF, as the seller does not need to pay for freight and insurance. One of the most important advantages of using incoterms is the fact that there is no misunderstanding of the responsibilities of the exporter and the importer.

Incoterms are classified by groups that include Group E, F, C, and D. Certain incoterms are used universally for any type of transport, whereas some are used specifically for inland waterway transport. More detailed explanations of each term can be found in the appendix.

Issuing the Purchase Order

Purchase orders (POs) are an important function in controlling business purchases. In this section, we will define what a PO is, describe the information it includes, and explain the key steps in the process of issuing a PO.

Information on a Purchase Order

A PO officially confirms the importer's order from the exporter. It is a document that is sent from the importer to the exporter authorizing the purchase of the goods or services. A purchase order contains important information for both parties. While there are many variations, purchase orders generally will include the name of the importing company purchasing the goods or services, the date, a description and quantity of the goods or services, the agreed upon price, a delivery address, payment information, the invoice address and a PO number.

The Purchase Order Process

There are four steps in the creation of the purchase order.

Step 1: The importer creates a purchase requisition. The creation of a PO starts with a purchase requisition, which is a document created by the importer and submitted to the finance department of the importer's company. In this step, the importer is not actually ordering anything but getting the approval to do so. The key difference between the purchase requisition and a PO is that the requisition is asking for permission and the order is about purchasing.

Step 2: The importer issues the PO. Once the purchasing department approves the requisition, it issues the PO to the exporter. In effect, POs formally place the order with the exporter.

Step 3: The exporter approves, rejects, or submits the PO. The exporter should review the PO thoroughly, paying close attention to the accuracy of the quantities specified, the prices agreed upon and the total amount due. Once the exporter approves the purchase order, usually via email, the prepare the goods or services to be delivered.

Step 4: The importer records the purchase order. The final step in the purchase order process involves the importer recording the PO. Filing purchase orders is a good habit in case of a future audit.

Once these four steps in the purchase order process are complete, the exporter arranges for the goods or services to be delivered and possibly inspected. Thereafter, the exporter issues an invoice to the importer, payment is made and the transaction is completed.

Export Financing

When dealing with the issue of export finance, more detail will be given in the following chapters. There are four general methods that exporters can use when negotiating the payment. The four main methods of payment are, cash in advance, open account (credit), letters of credit, and drafts. Exporters favor receiving cash in advance before they ship the goods. This avoids the risk of the importer not paying. Importers favor open account which allows them to sell the imported goods and acquire the revenue to repay the exporter.

Appointing an Agent

An agent is similar to a distributor in that they are a middleman. An agent does not take title to the exported goods and provides fewer services that a distributor would. The agent's role is to get orders and earn a commission for services rendered. For example, suppose ABC company is an import/export agent headquartered in Los Angeles. ABC is aware that XYZ International manufactures high quality shoes in Japan. ABC knows a big-name department store is looking to purchase these shoes. ABC is the middleman, bringing the buyer and seller together but not taking title to the goods and not providing any of the services that a distributor may perform. Global business has two main types of agents: the first is the traditional import/export agent. This person works in the country where the product is produced. The agent may identify a producer in the U.S. and look to represent that producer in a foreign market. The second type is a broker who is an independent agent bringing buyers and sellers together. A broker differs from the traditional import/export agent in that they do not represent any company. Instead, they are hired to bring together various deals.

Procuring the Order

Order procurement is the process in which goods may be stored, packing the orders, and shipping the product to the importer. In general, order procurement is everything that happens after the PO is issued by the importer up to the point they receive that order. The exporter can handle procurement in-house, outsource to a third party, dropship, or combine methods.

Arranging Insurance for Shipment

The need for export cargo insurance, known as marine insurance, often differs from exporter to exporter. The exporter is obligated to insure the cargo in the CIF incoterm, or the exporter may choose not to insure the cargo at their own risk in the DDU and DDP incoterms. The reason why exporters should buy marine insurance is to prevent financial loss if the goods are lost during transportation to the port of destination. Marine insurance is a class of property insurance that insures exported goods while in transit against loss or damage arising from perils associated with the navigation of the sea, air and subsequent land and inland waterways.

Booking Freight

Freight brokers work with exporters and transportation companies to help them move cargo and in return, receive a commission for their services. Freight brokers match cargos with carriers. They can be an individual or a company that matches exporters with specific transportation services. They are responsible for matching authorized and reliable carriers to the exporters and coordinating all the shipping needs for the exporter. When an exporter has a truckload of goods get to the ship, freight brokers find the transportation that can get that cargo to a specific location by way of a motor carrier. They will also negotiate the prices between the exporter and the carrier and make any necessary adjustments to the shipping service in order to get the job done.

Sending Documents

A single international transaction can involve up to 15 documents. In order to have a successful transaction, all required documents must be completed and submitted to clear the shipping and customs processes. The number of required documents is dependent on which countries are involved in the transaction. Freight forwarders and customs brokers can be of assistance, but the information must be accurately reported by the exporter. To find the requirements for a target country, U.S. exporters may consult with their partners or the U.S. embassy in the target country. More detail on specific documents can be found in the appendix.

Dispatch of Goods

Transporting goods from the port of origin to the port of destination is one of the many services provided by freight forwarding firms. The freight forwarder is the middleman between the transportation service and the exporter. They arrange the entire transaction including the storage and shipment of the goods if requested. Freight forwarders contract with transportation carriers to move the goods. The carriers use a variety of shipping modes including ships, planes, trucks and railroads and often use multiple modes for a single shipment. For example, the freight forwarder may arrange to have a cargo moved from the manufacturer to an airport by truck. Flown to the destination city, and then moved from the airport to the shipping line.

Customs Clearance

The procedures at the final stage of the import/export transaction are known as customs clearance. Export customs clearance includes all the procedures that must be followed in order to export a specified good to the importing country. These procedures include but are not limited to obtaining any export license or other official authorization to export the goods. Although exporting is an economic activity encouraged by most governments, exporters must pay attention to restrictions on certain items. Similarly, when exporting weapons and ammunition, it is necessary to obtain permission from the authorities of the exporting country. These clearances may be obtained through the freight forwarding company. An exporter's freight forwarder may work together with a customs broker in a foreign country in order to help facilitate issues with an export transaction. The customs broker will identify the documents to be collected for the transaction. As experts in the field, customs brokers help navigate the sea of changing regulations an understand the specifics of importing related to particular commodities.

Pricing in International Trade

Pricing for exports is distinctly different from pricing in the domestic market. With many unknown variables present in the international market, using a uniform price throughout the world is unrealistic. Many times, global trade associations and cartels will have posted prices that are not subject to negotiations. High price markups are common when there is little competition and the product is more differentiated. Typically, a high markup is used for medicine, computers, industrial equipment and telecommunications equipment. Low-priced exports are common where much competition is present whether it be textiles, food or cars. Aside from supply and demand, the exchange rate in both countries can affect the flow of imports and exports. Depreciation of the home currency leads to more exports to foreign buyers who have more purchasing power, whereas appreciation of the home currency gives local importers more purchase power and will increase import.

Export Price Calculation

When calculating the export price, there are two steps involved. The first step is known as the Landed Price, the second is the distributor's and retailer's price.

Calculating the Landed Price

When an exporter mentions his or her landed price, it usually involves the total cost once the export product has reached the importer's warehouse. Total landed costs include the original cost of the product, any brokerage fees to obtain it, the logistics fees, the shipping costs charged by the transport company, customs, taxes, marine and other insurances, the cost to convert currency charged by the currency broker or bank, any crating costs involved, and handling fees. The more the exporter can reduce any of these costs, the lower the final selling price and the greater the profit margin.

Calculating the Distributor's and Retailer's Price

It is generally accepted that each industry has a standard markup when calculating from cost to market price. The potential exporter is best advised to research the standard for the industry they intend to do business in and determine beforehand the profit margin they can expect.

Although it is customary for the exporter to charger a higher price during the first transactions and, then, to progressively reduce the price, there are four alternative approaches to pricing in an export market that include cost-based pricing, marginal pricing, skimming vs. penetration, and demand-based pricing.

Cost-Based Pricing

The most common form of export pricing is based on an orientation to cost. In this pricing approach, a markup will be determined first. The cost-based price will cover cost plus profit (the markup). The markup rate could be based on the desired return on investment with the understanding that the industry may have a standard, fixed markup to begin with.

Marginal Pricing

In marginal pricing, the price covers any additional cost to produce the exported product. When an exporter has excess or unused manufacturing capacity, the cost to produce extra units may be very different than the market price. It does not cover the total cost to produce the product but only any additional variable costs such as labor, raw materials, and utilities. As a result, the product may be sold at a lower price in the export market. The exporter who approaches pricing in this manner should be aware that international dumping laws prohibit a marginal price. Dumping occurs when manufacturers export a product to another country at a price below the normal global market price.

Skimming vs Penetration

Skimming is charging a premium price in the export market. This method is used when there are few competitors and a unique product. Typically, where an exporter has a niche market granted by a government license, skimming can be found. The target market is usually composed of high-income consumers and price inelastic demand.

Penetration pricing charges a lower price to enter the target market and gain market share. This method assumes higher volume will cover costs and lead to higher profits. For example, Sony entered the U.S. television market by charging a lower price than any other U.S. manufacturer. As a result, sales grew dramatically for Sony televisions. Eventually, Sony's brand was so well established, that it could introduce a top-of-the-line color television at much higher prices.

Demand-Based Pricing

Under this approach, to determine export prices the exporter will base the price on what buyers are willing to pay for the product or service. The key to this approach is market surveys which help supply the data that identifies the level of demand for the product or service. Once supplied with market survey data the exporter generally establishes the range of prices acceptable to buyers. With the introduction of the internet, market surveys are more inexpensive than ever.

To be competitive in an export market does not always mean to have the lowest price in the industry. If a product is superior or unique, it commands a higher price, especially if there is brand identification. For example, Rolex watches and Apple smartphones, despite their high prices, generate large sales volume globally due to brand recognition. Buyers feel a strong desire for these products and for which there are few or no good substitutes. On the other hand, where consumers are sensitive to changes in price, rebates and other discounts can revive declining sales.

PART 4

Financing Trade

CHAPTER 6

Methods of Payment in Transaction Financing

When dealing with the issue of payment, the exporter's motives differ from those of the importer. Exporters favor receiving payment as soon as the order is made and ideally before they ship the goods. Their main concern is failure to be paid by the importer. On the other hand, importers favor receiving the goods as soon as possible, while delaying payment as long as possible, ideally after the goods are sold. This delay offers them the opportunity to raise the funds to repay the exporter. The importer's main concern is that the exporter will fail to deliver or to deliver on time. Methods of payment can be structured so they benefit the importer more than the exporter and vice versa. For example, cash in advance favors the exporter since they receive payment as soon as possible. On the other hand, open account financing gives the advantage to the importer since they receive title to the shipment before taking the payment out of working capital.

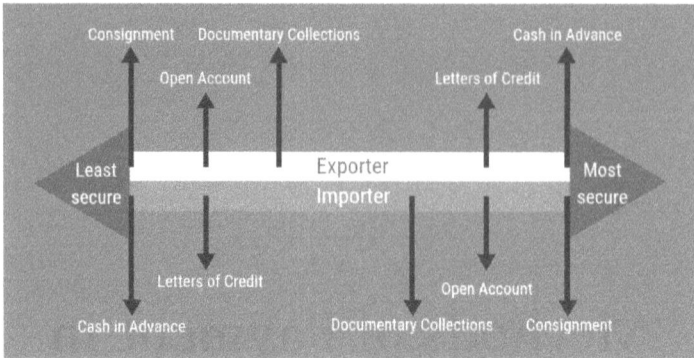

Figure 6.1 Methods of Payment

iContainers. "International Payment Methods." *IContainers*, 7 Feb. 2019, www.icontainers. com/help/international-payment-methods/.

Main Methods of Payment

Cash in Advance

Cash in advance means the payment will be sent before the shipment leaves the exporter's warehouse, usually via wire transfer. The payment can be put to immediate use, and there is no coordination required with banks or other intermediaries. This method of payment is most often used when exporters are confronted with three conditions. First, when faced with a new customer unknown to the exporter, cash in advance serves to reduce the uncertainty they will be paid. Second, during periods of political instability in the importer's country, cash in advance reduces the risk the shipment will be lost to foreign belligerents. Third, cash in advance is often used when the exporter manufactures goods that are unique and made to order for the importer. By requesting cash in advance it reduces the risk the importer may cancel the order before the goods are shipped leaving the exporter with unfinished goods that are unique to the importer. Liquidating this order becomes problematic for the exporter. For the importer, since cash in advance may come from working capital, it can create cash flow problems. Exporters asking for these kind of payment terms may not look competitive as importers will refuse payment until the merchandise is received and inspected.

Documentary Collections (Drafts)

A documentary collection (D/C), also known as a draft, is one of the most common methods of payment in international trade. Two banks are used to facilitate the process, one in the exporter's country and one in the importer's country. The draft can be drawn in either domestic or foreign currency. This method is a compromise between open account and the letter of credit financing. The fee for a D/C is usually fixed by the bank. Whereas an L/C will take a percentage of the transaction.

There are three functions for drafts. First, they present clear evidence of a financial obligation on the part of the importer. Second, they offer reduced financing costs when compared to the letter of credit. Third, a time draft can be a financial product. For example, an exporter who creates a time draft with an importer may be able to be paid earlier when the draft is converted by the bank into a banker's acceptance.

The procedure is as follows:

1. Both parties agree to the terms of the sale. The seller arranges the shipment with all the necessary documents and submits them to the remitting bank, with instructions on payment.
2. The remitting bank then sends the documents to the collecting bank in the importer's country
3. The collecting bank will then contact the importer for payment with one of two terms: document against payment (D/P) or documents against acceptance (D/A). If D/P, the importer must pay the collecting bank to receive the documents and title to

the shipment. The collecting bank then submits the payment to the remitting bank to pay the seller. If D/A, the collecting bank releases the documents on acceptance of the draft. Once the draft matures, the buyer makes payment to the collecting bank who then remits it to the seller with title and shipment is made.

Open Account

An open account method of payment creates a contract in which the exporter extends trade credit to the importer with the promise that payment is made within an agreed period of time. In accounting terms, the exporter creates the importer's liability as an accounts receivable. Once the seller sends the goods and all required documents, the payment is normally received in 30 to 120 days. It should be noted that in some countries accounts receivable are expected to give longer terms, sometimes up to 180 days. One disadvantage of this method is that it comes at a risk to exporters as it exposes them to an increased risk of default from their importer. On the other hand, by delaying payment the importer has the advantage to make sales and generate income to pay back the seller.

Open account financing is usually done between companies and their subsidiaries. Open account terms, in general, have recently become more popular with the surge in global trade. The increased use in open account terms is due to several reasons. First, credit reports are now more available than ever to verify the creditworthiness of the importers. These reports are available through commercial credit agencies, banks and public agencies. Second, more businesses are familiar with the terms and practices of global trade. Third, open account has become more popular due to surge in global trade itself.

The open account method of payment offers several benefits to the importer and exporter. First, it provides both greater flexibility in completing the transaction. When importers are allowed the additional time to resell and generate income to repay the exporter, they preserve working capital to generate additional business. Second, since there are no bank's fees to be paid, open account payments often come with lower transaction costs.

It should be noted there are significant disadvantages to used open account financing. The exporter is exposed to default risk by the importer because they are exposed to the risk of slow or late payment. Another disadvantage to the exporter is the exposure they will encounter to government currency controls. Most often in developing countries the importing government attempts to conserve hard currencies in payment for imports. As a solution, they will place controls on how many invoices the importers may pay every month.

Consignment

Consignment sales done across borders work the same as they would domestically. In this case, the exporter ships the goods overseas and does not transfer title or receive payment until the goods are sold by the importer. The importer (distributor) is obligated the pay the exporter only after they themselves receive payment from their buyer. This method is the riskiest for exporters, as there is no guaranteed timeline between shipment and repayment. Consignment sales are not commonly used in exporting but can be a way for sellers to phase out old products and reduce holding costs.

Countertrade

Countertrade is a non-cash method of payment typically used by large corporations. Like a barter transaction, it requires a double coincidence of wants. A countertrade contract may oblige the exporter to export a specified quantity of goods from the importing country in exchange for payment in a different specified quantity of goods.

Forms of Countertrade

Clearinghouse

A clearinghouse arrangement is a form of barter in which both parties agree to buy a certain amount of goods from each other. To do so a ratio of one product to another product is established and accounts are set up for them to credit and debit each other as needed. When the agreement matures, the parties settle in merchandise.

Buy-Back Transaction (Compensation Agreement)

In a buy-back transaction or compensation agreement, a firm sells or licenses technology. This may include the construction of a separate plant. The firm then agrees to purchase over a given number of years a certain amount of the output of the technology or the plant. The duration of the agreement may range from a few years to 30 years or longer. Since the agreement may involve transfer of proprietary technology, it is extremely important to protect, patent and trademark.

Counter-purchase Trade Agreement

As in the compensation agreement, counter-purchase consists of two parallel transactions. In a counter purchase, a company sells good to an importer, promising to counter-purchase from the importer some other specified goods. In the first transaction, the exporter sells goods to the importer with the promise to purchase other goods from the importer. The counter-purchase transaction is often short term (3-5 years).

Offset Transaction

An offset is a transaction where the exporter allows the importer, generally a foreign government to offset the cost of purchasing its product. Such transactions are mainly used for high-ticket items such as defense-related sales, commercial aircraft, or sales of expensive high-tech products. Offset transactions are most often used by many importing countries as a way to compensate for large hard currency payment resulting from the purchase. They may also create investment and employment opportunities in the importing country.

References

"International Trade Finance." *Tutorialspoint*, www.tutorialspoint.com/international_finance/international_trade_finance.htm.

Methods of Payment. (n.d.). Retrieved from https://www.export.gov/article?id=Trade-Finance-Guide-Methods-of-Payment.

CHAPTER 7

Letter of Credit: The Basics

Parties to Letters of Credit

As mentioned earlier, both parties to an international transaction will have concerns about how the transaction will be completed. Importers who pay in advance for a shipment but have issues with the quality and when it arrives. The exporter may send a shipment and have issues as to when payment will be made. Letters of credit (L/C) are often used to relieve these concerns and protect the interests of both parties.

Definition

To ensure the exporter is paid, the exporter or other beneficiary may seek the superior credit standing of a large bank. The L/C provides this function. The credit in the L/C is addressed to the seller, written and signed by the opening bank which acts on behalf of the buyer. In an L/C, the bank promises that it will pay or accept drafts if the seller conforms exactly to the conditions set forth in the letter. Most L/Cs will state in their conditions that the exporter must submit, together with the draft, other documents such as the bill of lading, the insurance certificate, and the invoices.

With the L/C, the opening bank substitutes its own commitment to pay when its customer, the importer, does not. Although it is not in reality a guarantee, the L/C serves the same purpose, that is, the opening bank assures payment to the exporter as long as the exporter complies with the stated conditions.

Advantages to the Exporter

An L/C offers most of the advantages to an exporter. When the importer opens a letter of credit in favor of the exporter, there may be substantial advantages to the exporter such as: eliminating credit and political risks.

Eliminating Credit Risk. When payment is assured by a respectable commercial bank, the exporter no longer needs to rely on the ability of the importer to make payment. If the opening bank is credible, the exporter can be certain that all invoice amounts due will be paid on time as long as they adhere to the terms of the letter. If the importer defaults in making payment, the opening bank will reimburse the exporter.

Reduces or Eliminates Political Risk. Because an exporter who ships open account always faces the danger that payment may be delayed due to political causes, the L/C reduces but does not eliminate these risks. There is always the danger that the government of the importing country may cancel the importer's license or take some other actions that prevents payment. In addition, political disturbances such as civil war and unrest may prevent payment. Furthermore, the government of the importing country may get into financial difficulties and may place a moratorium on all outgoing foreign payments.

When an L/C is opened by an importer at a local bank, the political risks are reduced but not eliminated. Even if a country imposes new restrictions, open L/C's of its commercial banks are usually exempt. A country's international credit standing may be severely damaged when its commercial banks fail to do this.

Reduces need for Credit Checking. An exporter who is the beneficiary of an L/C by a reputable bank needs to devote minimal time checking on the credit of the importer. The major responsibility to investigate the importer's creditworthiness is assumed by the opening bank. The opening bank located in the importer's country has a much easier time evaluating creditworthiness of the importer than a more distant exporter.

The exporter knows all requirements for payment. An L/C stipulates exactly the requirements for the seller to get payment. When the exporter is the beneficiary of an L/C, the letter has a clear an unambiguous description of all the terms. The exporter has full confidence that, in due course, when all the steps are taken to meet the documentary requirements, they will receive payment.

Protection on Preshipment Risks. A manufacturer under contract to produce a unique and specialized piece of equipment for the importer faces the risk of cancellation of a contract before shipment. Early cancellation may involve substantial out-of-pocket expenditures to the exporter. Since the product is unique to the importer, the exporter may have trouble selling it in the market and may suffer substantial losses.

Facilitates Financing. When an importer opens the L/C, it is the importer's credit line at the opening bank that is used. The exporter looks to the bank for payment. The opening bank in turn looks to the importer for immediate or eventual reimbursement.

When shipments are made using an L/C, it facilitates the creation of a banker's acceptance. Furthermore, sound credit backing and clear-cut source of payment is identified. This ease of credit backing and source of payment makes commercial banks especially ready to provide needed financing.

In addition to needed financing, a manufacturer or exporter often requires a loan to finance the production process or to purchase the goods from a supplier. Since an L/C with an exporter as the beneficiary guarantees payment by the opening bank, it may facilitate short-term financing for the exporter to purchase the product from the supplier.

Advantages to the Importer

Although an L/C offers more advantages to the exporter, there are advantages for the importer that address their greatest concerns, mainly receiving the shipment from the exporter.

Payment only after compliance. The importer who opens an L/C with a reputable bank can be confident that payment to the exporter will be made only after the exporter has complied with all the stipulations. Consequently, the importer will be certain the goods are actually shipped on a certain date. If the importer doubts the exporter's ability to ship, the quality they demand, the importer may include an inspection certificate as part of the required documentation.

Expert Examination of Documents. Once the exporter submits the required documents to the opening bank, trained clerks with many years of experience usually examine them. They will ensure that the documents agree with the credit and the bill of lading. This means that what appears on a bill of lading also appears on the commercial invoice as well as the L/C. The importer therefore is assured that each document is carefully inspected and receives the product they agreed to purchase. If the bank clerks detect an important discrepancy, the exporter as well as the importer are notified. Before the L/C can be paid, the discrepancy must be eliminated by all three.

Expanded Sources of Supply. Many exporters are only willing to sell against cash in advance or letters of credit as a matter of their business policy. The importer who offers an L/C from a reputable bank, therefore may be able to expand the number of suppliers who are willing to ship to them.

Easier Financing. It had previously been mentioned that an L/C involving a time draft had been especially easy to create a banker's acceptance. Because of this, an importer may find financing under an L/C easier to obtain than under other methods of payment. An exporter who knows they will be paid by a credible opening bank, the exporter may offer better terms to the importer especially terms compared to open account.

No Tie-Up of Working Capital. With a cash in advance transaction, the importer may tie up needed working capital to finance the transaction. When an L/C is used as an alternative, the problem of working capital is solved. The importer is required to pay only after shipment. Furthermore, opening an L/C involves bank charges but be less than the interest foregone by having to pay the exporter at an earlier date.

Parties to the L/C Transaction

If an L/C is required, it must be stated in the sales contract between the importer and exporter. Since most letters of credit are opened by the importer, payment terms are usually included in the contract at the exporter's request. In this case, the party in whose favor the letter is opened (the exporter) is called the beneficiary.

Account Party

Most often it is up to the importer to find an opening bank that is willing to create a letter of credit. The applicant for a letter of credit, most often the importer, is referred to as the account party.

Opening Bank

The bank responsible for opening an L/C on behalf of the importer or exporter is known as the opening bank. By issuing a credit, the opening bank assumes full responsibility for payment if the importer defaults. The credit of the opening bank therefore is substituted for the account party provided the proper documents have been presented.

Advising Bank

A copy of the L/C is often mailed directly to the exporter, who is the beneficiary. The exporter then presents their draft and documents to a local bank willing to accept the draft. This bank is called the "advising bank." Its responsibility is to inform the beneficiary that the letter of credit has been opened in their favor. The advising bank advises the letter of credit to the beneficiary without responsibility on its part. On the other hand, it may still be held liable for such things as erroneous notification of the L/C terms if this results in a loss to the exporter.

Paying Bank

The advising bank may also act as the paying bank. This occurs when the advising bank is authorized to pay the exporter's draft when presented and accompanied by the proper documentation. The documents must include a bill of lading and a commercial invoice. In any case, the paying bank after having paid the beneficiary will be reimbursed by the opening bank provided the proper documentation is presented. In effect, the paying bank acts as the agent for the opening bank.

Confirming Bank

Frequently, the exporter may request an additional guarantee of payment from another bank who will add its credit to the original letter of credit. In this case, the additional bank is known as the "confirming" bank. When it adds its own name to the credit, the confirming bank accepts the risk of default by the importer as well as the opening bank. For accepting this risk, the confirming bank charges a fee that is usually paid by the importer. A confirmed letter of credit is considered very safe from the exporter's point of view, since two banks are obliged to pay.

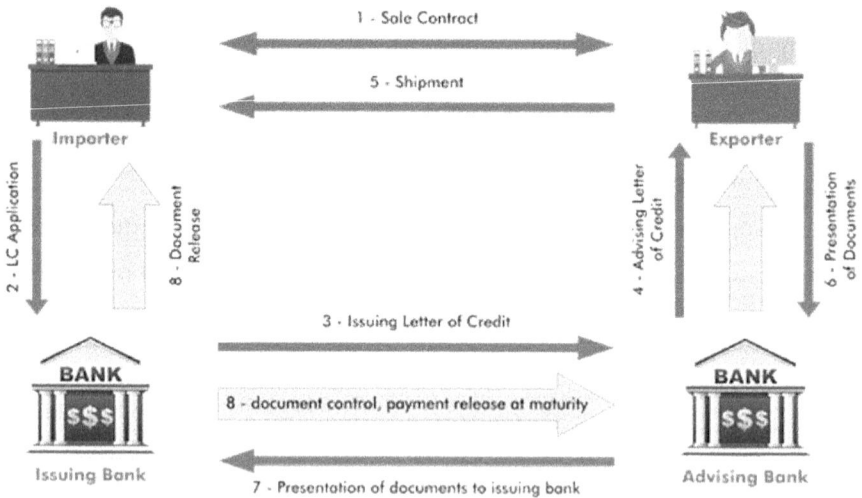

Figure 7.1 The Route of a Letter of Credit

Opening of a Letter of Credit

An L/C is usually opened any time after the sales contract has been signed but before shipment of the goods. The exporter will usually request the importer to arrange for the opening of the credit as soon as possible after the signing of the sales contract. If there is any change to the term of the credit, the exporter and importer are protected when the L/C is known as irrevocable. In an irrevocable L/C, no changes are permitted without the approval of the three parties to the transaction: the opening bank, the exporter and the importer. If changes are required, all three parties must agree. Irrevocable letters of credit protect the three parties from unexpected changes in terms.

Requirements for the Account Party

When requesting the bank to open an L/C, the account party, most often the importer, must submit and sign an application as well as a signed letter of credit agreement. Through the application, the account party will give the bank exact requirements such as, the manner of the notification to the beneficiary, the amount, the tenure, required documents and expiration dates. The requirements of the application should conform with the underlying sales contract in order that the L/C will be opened exactly as required. For example, it must be specified the type of marine insurance that is required. If it remains unspecified, the bank is free to accept any coverage offered. Vague or ambiguous requirements must be avoided.

The application calls for a general description of the merchandise to be shipped. Inserting unnecessary details increases the possibility of the opening bank finding discrepancies and may cause disputes concerning who is responsible.

The Letter of Credit Agreement

The importer, or the account party, opens the L/C. In the agreement, the importer states it will provide the bank with funds to pay for sight drafts as they are submitted under the credit agreement. The importer usually will agree to pay bank fees and interest charges.

Requirements to the Opening Bank

After the application and the letter of credit agreement are submitted to the opening bank, the credit is typed and sent to the beneficiary, either directly or through the advising bank. Once the beneficiary receives the irrevocable L/C, the liability of the opening bank to pay provided the proper documents are submitted is established.

Letter of Credit Contents

The information most often found in an L/C is as follows:

1. Place and Date of Issuance
2. Names of the Account Party & Beneficiary
3. A general description of the merchandise. This usually indicates the quantity of merchandise to be shipped.
4. The tenure of the draft. Here the exporter indicates whether a site or time draft will be drawn on the opening of the paying bank. In the case of a time draft, a stated number of days will be specified.
5. The name of the bank on whom the drafts may be drawn
6. The ports of origin and destination
7. A list of the exact documents that will need to be attached to the draft. Usually, an L/C covering the movement of goods requires

the presentation of a negotiable, onboard clean bill of lading that conveys title to the goods being shipped. When additional documents are required, they usually include the certificate of insurance, the commercial invoice, consular invoice, inspection certificate and others depending on the transaction.

8. An expiration date for the credit. There are usually two dates stated on the L/C that clarify the latest time at which certain actions must be taken and the latest shipping date for onboard bill of lading. This includes the final expiration date that gives the time in which the draft and documents must be paid to the paying bank. Usually, the final expiration date is a few days after the last permissible shipping date.

9. A commitment by the opening bank that states the drafts drawn on it by the exporter will be honored provided all the conditions are met.

10. Whether the L/C is revocable or irrevocable.

References

O'Connor, B. (2019, January 11). Letter of Credit: What It Is and How It Works. Retrieved from https://www.fundera.com/blog/letter-of-credit.

CHAPTER 8

Methods of Financing

Short Term Financing

Discounting

Draft discounting is a financial operation where the owner of a time draft sells the ownership to a bank in exchange for cash. Since this is a time draft, some interest will be deducted by the bank from the face value before the maturity date. This short-term method of financing means that the bank becomes the owner legally of the draft. The discounting bank then collects payment from the importer as the draft matures. Discounting a draft is an effective and useful method for the financing of a transaction especially when the exporter is in need of working capital. The maximum term of most drafts discounted in this way is six months.

Banker's Acceptances

A banker's acceptance provides a bridge between the importer and the exporter typically when they do not have a preestablished relationship. A banker's acceptance is created when an importer wants to finance the purchase of goods from a foreign vendor. To do this, the importer creates a time draft and presents it to their bank. When the bank accepts the draft, the bank discounts it and gives the importer the cash needed to pay the exporter. The acceptance is a legally binding obligation by the accepting bank to pay the stated amount at the time of maturity. Typical maturities range from 30 to 180 days. The acceptance is then sold by the bank to investors in short-term financial markets. On or before the maturity date of the accepted draft, the face amount of the acceptance must be paid by the importer to the investor who owns the acceptance. Investors consider banker's acceptances as very safe investments.

Sequence of Steps in the Creation of A Banker's Acceptance

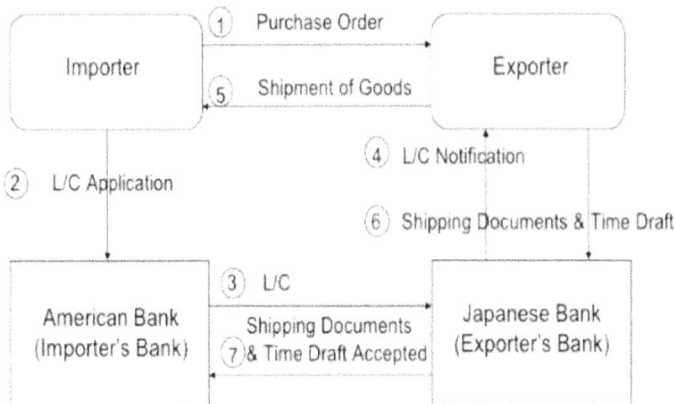

Figure 8.1 Creating a Banker's Acceptance

Factoring

Factoring is a financial transaction in which exporter sells the accounts receivable they have created for their importer to a third party referred to as the "factor," usually at a discount. An exporter sometimes factors its receivables to raise short term working capital. There are usually three parties involved: the first party is the factor or the company who purchases an exporter's receivables. The second party is the exporter. The third-party is usually the importer who has the financial liability to pay the exporter at some future date. If the factor purchases the receivables "without recourse," the factor must bear any loss if the importer does not pay the exporter's accounts receivable. On the other hand, if the factor purchases the receivables "with recourse," the factor has the legal right to collect the unpaid invoice from the importer.

Line of Credit

A line of credit is a preset amount of money that a bank agrees to lend to the exporter. The exporter can draw from the line when capital is needed up to the maximum amount. The amount drawn down from the line of credit is subject to interest charges. A line of credit is similar to a credit card in that it is flexible in its borrowing. The exporter can borrow any part of a credit line again once it has been repaid. Lines of credit are usually unsecured, meaning there is no collateral required. Once the money is borrowed from the line of credit, interest is charged and minimum payments are usually required.

Credit Card

While not an ideal source of funds, credit cards can be utilized for capital needs of an export/import business. They often charge high interest rates and late fees that incur further costs. Nonetheless, credit cards may be one of few options available to a new exporter. Many lenders will not extend lines of credit or loans without an established business and credit history and income stream. When shopping, it is possible to search for the lowest available interest rates. Some banks may even offer promotional rates that forgo any interest for the first year or two. With a sound business plan and agreements with foreign buyers, credit cards can be successfully used to finance an international transaction.

Purchase Order Financing

Purchase order financing is a short-term method for exporters to raise cash to fulfill single or multiple orders from customers. Exporters at times may find there is not enough working capital available to cover the cost of a new order being placed by an importer. Rather than turn the order down the exporter may resort to this form of financing. In this method of financing, the exporter pays its supplier using the importer's purchase order. The financing is in advance of the importers payment and may not be for the entire amount of the supplier. In some cases, exporters may qualify for 100% financing. The purchase order finance company collects the invoice from the importer and makes its profits by charging the exporter various fees which may be taken out of the amount of the collected invoice.

Warehouse Financing

Warehouse financing is a form of inventory financing in which loans are made on the basis of an inventory of goods that are held as collateral for loans. The goods may be held in what is known as public warehouses that are approved by a lender such as a bank. They also may be held in what is known as field warehouses located in the exporters facilities but controlled by an independent third party. A bank that is usually engaged in this type of financing designates a third party known as the warehouse manager. This manager issues a warehouse receipt to the borrower (in this case the exporter) and certifies the quantity and quality of the goods while releasing them to the exporter ahead of payment. In this way, warehouse financing enables the exporter to obtain financing on more favorable terms than a line of credit. The reason for this is the fact that the loans are secured by the goods in inventory.

Using L/Cs for Short-Term Financing

In many situations, the exporter will be the middleman between the supplier and the importer. The challenge to the exporter will be payment in advance to the supplier. This is especially problematic when the exporter and the supplier are new to each other and the supplier is not willing to offer open account financing to the exporter. Letters of credit have many forms such as assignment of proceeds, time letter of credit, transferable letter of credit and back-to-back letter of credit, all of which will address this problem.

Assignment of Proceeds

When an exporter acts primarily as a middleman, they will have the L/C opened in their favor as the beneficiary. A problem may arise when the exporters supplier requires some form of payment before releasing the goods. If the exporter does not have adequate financial resources, they must use short term financing. To assure the supplier's payment, the exporter may be able to transfer funds to the manufacturer. It is known as an assignment of proceed. The main benefit to the exporter is the fact that, given an L/C opened their, they will induce their supplier to ship the exported goods.

Time Letter of Credit

A time letter of credit can be used as a short-term method of financing. It calls for the creation of an acceptance draft, known as a usance, to be drawn on or accepted by either the opening or paying bank. If the letter of credit is denominated in the importer's currency, the time draft is usually drawn on the paying bank. On the other hand, if the credit is denominated in the exporter's currency, the time draft is drawn on the paying bank. If all documents are in order, the drawee bank creates the acceptance draft. If the exporter has the promise from a reputable accepting bank, it can be confident that it will be paid at the maturity date of the acceptance. When the acceptance is created, it is based on the strength of a promise from the opening bank, which relies on the importer for ultimate payment.

Discounting the Acceptance

An exporter facing cash flow problems may not be willing to wait until the acceptance maturity date before receiving payment. In this case, the exporter generally asks the accepting bank to discount the acceptance. This means the exporter will receive the face value of the draft minus discount charges immediately. Since there is an active market for acceptances, most banks are generally willing to discount their own acceptances at prevailing market rates.

Transferable Letter of Credit

With a transferable L/C, the primary beneficiary (the exporter) can request the issuing bank to make all or part of the funds available to a one or more secondary beneficiaries. No L/C is transferrable unless specifically authorized by the bank who opens the credit. The exporter can delegate shipping responsibilities to its supplier, the secondary beneficiary, who receives payment as long as the shipments are made. It should be noted that a secondary beneficiary must be located in the same country as the original beneficiary unless otherwise permitted. A separate part of the L/C is made payable directly to the exporter and represents the profit from the transaction. One benefit of a transferable L/C is that it allows the exporter to keep the identity of the manufacturer hidden from the importer. When the documents that cover the transferred portion of the credit are received by the bank, it notifies the primary beneficiary. The primary beneficiary may then substitute his own invoice for that of the second beneficiary, the manufacturer.

Back-to-back Letter of Credit

Another method to which the beneficiary of an L/C can create short-term financing is the back-to-back L/C. When the exporter is the beneficiary of an irrevocable L/C, he may induce his bank to open a second similar credit on his behalf for the ultimate purpose of paying a supplier or manufacturer as the beneficiary. To create a back-to-back L/C, the exporter assigns the primary credit to his bank as collateral. The secondary credit is similar to the first except the amount may be lower because the exporter has deducted his profit. This arrangement gives maximum protection to the exporter's supplier, giving them an L/C that guarantees payment provided the supplier meets with all conditions.

References

Commercial Draft Discounting. Retrieved from http://www.boc. cn/en/cbservice/cb2/cb24/200806/t20080627 1320889.html

Woodruff, J. (2018, March 06). How Does a Banker's Acceptance Work? Retrieved from https://bizfluent.com/13709437/how-does-a-bankers-acceptance-work

Long Term Methods of Financing

Bank Financing

Small businesses often encounter difficulties and challenges when searching for funding. The owner may not have much business or credit history. Less than half of all small businesses make it past the third year. Survival rates for export-import businesses is generally higher, but they are still prone to risks that domestic businesses are not exposed to. Because of these inherent risks, banks are unlikely to extend start-up loans without collateral. For a bank to provide a loan, they will examine your business plan for quantifiable financial goals and how the loan is to be repaid. If the borrower has sufficient cash on hand and is backed by an experienced management team a loan may be approved.

There are two types of loans the bank may then extend:

Secured loan

A secured loan is one that is fixed to an asset that is used as collateral. The bank will lend an amount equal to or close to the value of the collateral. Anything the business owns, from land, buildings, cars, corporate securities or saving accounts may be used as collateral for the loan. Secured loans usually have a lower rate of interest.

Unsecured loan

With a history of good credit, business owners could apply for a personal or commercial loan with nothing but a signature as a guarantee of repayment. This this incurs greater risk to the bank in the way of repayments, such loans are typically subject to higher interest rates.

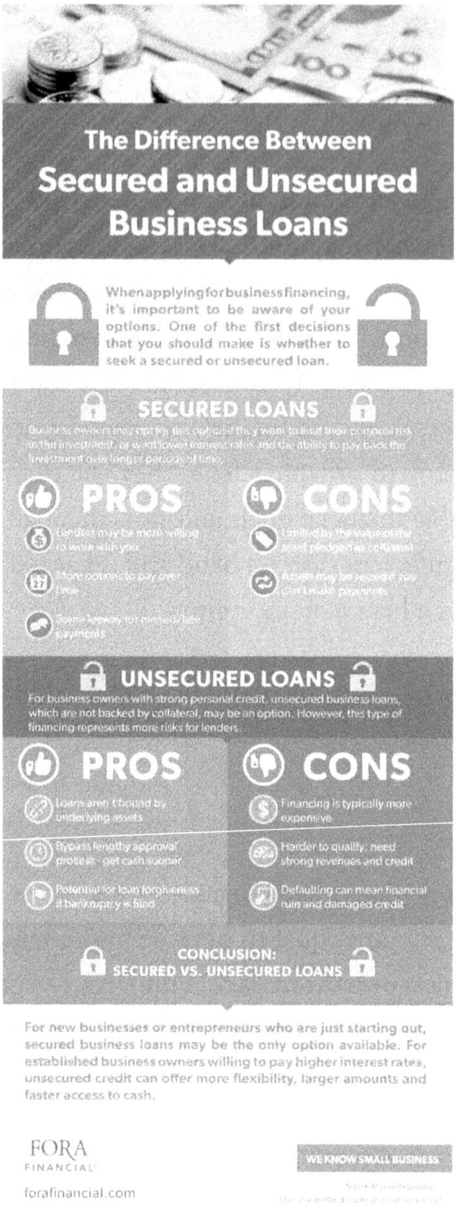

Figure 8.2 Secured vs Unsecured Loans

"Secured vs. Unsecured Business Loans: Fora Financial Blog." Fora Financial, Fora Financial, 3 Oct. 2019, www.forafinancial.com/blog/working-capital/secured-and-unsecured-business-loans/.

CHAPTER 9

Assistance Programs

U.S. Government Programs

The Export-Import Bank of the United States

T he **Export-Import (EXIM) Bank** is the only U.S. federal agency that exclusively was created to facilitate and finance U.S. exports. With the current trend of increased internationalization in the U.S., the bank's role continues to grow due to exports comprising a larger and growing share of the U.S. GDP. In addition, the volume of international trade has increased substantially with increased competition for export markets.

The role of the EXIM Bank is to supplement but not compete with private financing. It is historically more active in markets where the private finance sector has been reluctant to provide export financing.

The three main functions of the bank are to provide export credit insurance and guarantees to provide competitive financing for small businesses, and to negotiate to reduce subsidies and export credits. The EXIM Bank provides four major financing programs for exporters; Working Capital Guarantee Program, Export Credit Insurance, commercial loan guarantees, and direct loans.

The bank requires certain conditions before it provides assistance to U.S exporters. First condition is that the exports must include a minimum of 50% U.S. content. Second, the exports must not be related to military operations. Third, the exports must be produced in an environmentally friendly atmosphere and must not results in negative impacts to a foreign environment. Provided these conditions are met, the bank's financing decision is based upon the borrower's ability to repay the loan. To establish this ability, the exporter who applies for assistance must provide the bank with three years financials. There are four major export finance programs provided by the EXIM Bank for exporters: The Working Capital Guarantee Program, The Export Credit Insurance Program, Guarantees of Commercial Loans to Foreign Buyers and Direct Loans to Foreign Buyers.

Working Capital Guarantee Program (WGCP)

All export businesses must efficiently utilize their working capital to operate or expand. Because most banks are reluctant to make financing available due to small businesses due to limited collateral or because they have reached their bank's borrowing limits, the WCGP is intended to encourage banks to make loans. The loans may be used for variety of purposes such as purchasing inventory, financing overhead expenses or covering L/Cs. Eligible exporters such as small and middle-sized companies may apply to the EXIM Bank for a preliminary commitment for a guarantee. This commitment is a non-binding expression of interest from the EXIM Bank that indicates that the proposed trade transaction, as outlined in the EXIM's application, is of the type that may qualify for EXIM Bank support. A further detailed examination of the proposed transaction that will take place at the time of a final commitment application. Such an application would not be expected for a matter of months. In addition, the exporter's bank may also apply directly for authorization for the final guarantee. When applying, the EXIM Bank will specify the terms and conditions under which it will provide a guarantee to the exporter. The specifications can be used by the exporter to approach various potential lenders to secure the most competitive loans package. The major features of the WCGP include the following:

Qualified Exports. Eligible exports must be shipped from the U.S. and contain more than 50% U.S. content. In addition to being environmentally friendly, the exported items may not be military items or sold to military buyers.

Guarantee Coverage and Term of the Loan. In the case of default by the exporter, the EXIM Bank will guarantee 90% of the loan's principal up to the date of claim for payment. This assumes the lending bank with the guarantee has met all the terms and conditions of the guarantee agreement. In general, guaranteed loans have maturity of 12 months and are renewable.

Collateral and Borrowing Capacity. According to EXIM bank requirements, lenders must secure guaranteed loans with collateral. Some acceptable collateral would include export-related inventory, export-related accounts receivable, and other assets. For service companies, collateral may include the cost of engineering, design, or overhead. In general, exporters can borrow over 70% of their inventory and 90% of their accounts receivable.

Qualified Exporters and Lenders. To qualify for EXIM Bank loan guarantees, exporters must be located in the United States, show two years of successful financial statements, and have a positive net worth.

Financial statements should show the income stream necessary to repay the requested debt. Any public or private lender is eligible under the public program. The criteria for eligibility are determined on the basis of many factors. Some factors would include the lender's financial condition, experience with trade finance, and ability to manage asset-based loans.

Export Credit Insurance Program (ECIP)

One of the most popular programs of the EXIM Bank is the ECIP. Its purpose is to promote U.S. sales by exporters and to insure them against loss in the event of default by the foreign importer. The ECIP also enables exporters to more easily obtain financing since the proceeds of an ECIP policy can be readily assigned to the exporter's bank as collateral and guarantee of repayment. The EXIM Bank also offers a wide variety of policies to accommodate many different insurance needs of exporters and their banks.

Guarantees of Commercial Loans

The EXIM Bank provides credit worthy foreign buyers of U.S. exports with a guarantee to repay their private loans or line of credit. This program guarantees to cover 100% of the commercial and political risk. This coverage is available for medium and long-term transactions. Given the foreign buyer makes a cash payment of at least 15% they qualify for this treatment that includes equipment, services, and projects.

These guarantees help exporters and importers in a number of ways. A loan guarantee mitigates the risk of default with a particular buyer. Loan guarantees allow international buyers financing with U.S capital goods. EXIM loan guarantees make it easier and more secure to enter emerging markets. There are no limits on the transaction size.

Direct Loans

The EXIM Bank's direct loan program helps exporters secure competitive financing for their creditworthy international buyers. The loans may involve purchases of U.S. capital equipment and related services. The program provides fixed-rate financing for up to 12 years in general and 18 years for renewable energy projects. It also provides financing for the exporter's local costs up to 30%. These loans cover up to 85% percent of the export value when a cash payment is made for the difference.

Eligibility. The EXIM programs finance only the U.S. content of a transaction. It can do business in most markets, but it may limit financing for certain countries. The products must be shipped from the U.S. to a foreign buyer. There is no minimum or maximum limit to the size of the sale that may be financed with a direct loan. The program cannot support the export of anything with military applications.

Fees. The direct loan program requires a letter of interest that incurs a processing fee of $100. It will also include a commitment fee based of 0.5% of the unused portion of the loan. The interest rate is fixed during the term of the loan.

U.S. Small Business Administration

The U.S. Small Business Administration, or SBA, is a government agency that provides support with financing and counseling to U.S. entrepreneurs. The following financing options are offered by the SBA:

Export Working Capital Loans. This program allows small businesses such as exporters to apply for loans in advance of finalizing an export sale. With this loan program, exporters are given greater flexibility in negotiating payment terms with their buyers. The size of the loans can be up to $5 million and involve a turnaround of 5-10 business days. Lenders review and approve applications that they submit to the U.S. Capital Export Assistance Center location servicing the exporter's region. Lenders and borrowers can negotiate the interest, but it may not exceed the SBA maximum. Revolving lines of credit are given terms of 12 months or less. The SBA requires a personal guarantee from exporters with 20% or more ownership in their personal property. The proceeds can be used for purchasing inventory or raw materials to manufacture a product.

International Trade Loans. These loans provide long-term financing to exporters that are expanding due to increased export sales. Many times, the loan is used by exporters that have been adversely affected by imports and need to modernize to meet foreign competition. Exports can use international trade loans for construction, building, equipment, and working capital for export transactions. The maximum loan amount is $5 million, and the SBA guarantee is 90%. The interest rate is negotiable between lenders and borrowers, but it may not exceed the SBA maximum. Loan maturity can be 10 years for permanent working capital, up to 10 years for machinery and equipment and up 25 years for real estate.

Export Express Loans. This program may be used for revolving lines of credit and guarantees up to $250,000 to exporters seeking to expand export operations. The funds can be used for trade shows or standby letters of credit. To qualify, the exporter should be in business for at least one year.

Small Business Development Centers (SBDC)

SBDCs are sponsored by the SBA and can be found in all U.S. states and territories. The SBA typically partners with a local university to provide educational resources to entrepreneurs through the SBDCs. Since the SBDC's will employ third party expert consultants, the centers have the advantage of practical private sector knowledge combined with the educational capabilities of a learning institution.

U.S. Commercial Service (USCS)

The U.S. Department of Commerce houses the U.S. Commercial Service has field offices all over the world. While it does not offer financing, the Commercial Service provides a wealth of resources to new exporters. Under the parent organization, known as the International Trade Association, the Commercial Service supports exporters by providing a range of information on the importing country. This information comes in the form of reports prepared at international offices by local authorities. For example, the USCS can provide a report, known as the Country Commercial Guide, for exporters that wish to trade with Germany. In the guide, the commercial specialists help exporters identify trade opportunities, find local partners, promote products and services, obtain market research, and protect intellectual property rights. The Commercial Service trade specialists in 100 U.S. cities and in more than 80 countries work with exporters to help them increase their sales in new global markets. In their country reports, the commercial service provides a vast array of market information. Using Germany as an example, the market information will include: how to conduct business, what the exporter needs to know beforehand, Germany-related trade fairs, downloadable market research and business service providers.

Other Services for Exporters

Matching Service. Through the Gold Key program, the USCS provides help in finding potential overseas agents, distributors, sales reps, and business partners for U.S. exporters. They will arrange business meetings with qualified contacts such as local representatives, distributors, professional associations, government contacts and licensing or joint venture partners. The Gold Key program has a matching service that offers the following:

- Customized market and industry briefings with trade specialists
- Timely and relevant market research
- Appointments with prospective trade partners in key industry sectors
- Post-meeting debriefing with trade specialists and assistance with developing appropriate follow-up strategies
- Assistance with travel, accommodations, interpreter service and clerical support

Every year this service helps thousands of exporters to find the best opportunities for business all around the world.

Industry Reports. The service also provides industry reports on a selected industry sector prepared by industry specialists and free of charge. The reports include information as follows:

- Market Potential and Demand trends
- Market size and import stats
- Competition
- Market access
- Regulations and standards
- Distribution practices
- Best Sales Prospects
- End Users
- Key industry contacts

Using a source known as the Market Intelligence Database, the exporter can conduct a basic analysis of the import target market.

Customized Market Reports. Another of the available services is a customized market research where industry specialists prepare a report according to the specific exporter's needs. The reports will:

- Gauge the exporter's sales potential in the target market
- Choose the best new markets for the exporter's product or service
- Establish effective selling or distribution strategies in target markets
- Find the best channels for getting the export product to market
- Discover what factors influence the potential customers the most
- Identify the exporter's competitors in the target market
- Overcome potential market impediments, including quotas, tariffs, and regulations

Trade Shows. International trade shows are an excellent opportunity to find potential importers. The USCS provides and overview of trade shows in targeted countries. Their team of specialists provide specific information for relevant industry sectors.

State Government Assistance Programs

Data are available by the individual state or U.S. region for foreign trade information about individual countries.

State Trade Expansion Program (STEP)

Each U.S. state will have what is known as a State Trade Expansion program, or STEP. STEPs are designed to drive exports of businesses in the states that they service. These STEPs leverage their statewide network of trade promotion organizations to facilitate export promotion.

As an example, the California STEP serves a variety of industries including

- Information and communications tech
- Green Technologies
- Food and Agricultural products
- California Lifestyle Products
- Medical Equipment
- Scientific Instrumentation
- Transportation Equipment
- Industrial Machinery

To participate, the program establishes certain basic qualifications such as:

- Compliance with SBA size standards
- Have been in business for at least one year from the date in which assistance is provided
- Operation and incorporated in the United States
- Demonstrated understanding of the costs associated with exporting and doing business with foreign buyers including the costs of freight forwarding, customs brokers, packing, and shipping
- Exporting goods or services of U.S. origin or that have at least 51% or more U.S. content

Non-Profit Organizations

Many non-profit organizations exist for the sole purpose of promoting American small businesses and exporters. Aspiring entrepreneurs can receive assistance at little to no cost in the form of counseling to create effective international business plans.

SCORE

The Service Corps of Retired Executives (SCORE) provides a source of free business mentoring and free education to new businesses. As a resource partner of the SBA, score has helped entrepreneurs since 1964 through mentoring, workshops, and educational resources.

Mentoring

Exporters can access free confidential business mentoring in person at 300 local chapters or remotely via email, phone, and video. SCORE mentors who are experts in their related fields meet with exporters on an ongoing basis to provide continued advice and support.

Webinars and Courses on Demand

SCORE regularly offers free online workshops on export topics ranging from startup strategies to marketing and finance. Attendees watch live webinars or view recordings online on their own time. In addition, SCORE offers interactive courses on demand that the exporter can walk through each module at their own pace.

Library of Online Resources

Exporters can also benefit from SCORE's extensive collection of e-guides, templates, checklists, blogs, videos and more. It strives to provide the most relevant and current educational content to help small exporters and entrepreneurs succeed.

Local Events

Many local SCORE chapters hold free or low-cost in-person workshops and round table discussions covering a range of exporting topics.

State Regional Trade Groups

In the United States, there is multiple **State Regional Trade Groups** (SRTGs), each representing a different region of the U.S., such as the Northeast or Midwest. These associations typically help promote U.S food exports through marketing via trade missions/fairs. Some may even offer funding programs that will compensate businesses for a portion of their international marketing expenses. SRTGs such as the Western United States Agricultural Trade Association (WUSATA) will help exporters from the region. Their Global Product service helps create exposure to foreign markets, and their Fund Match program can reimburse up to 50% of eligible marketing expenses.

References

About Us. (n.d.). Retrieved from https://californiaexport.org/about/.

Get Financing. (n.d.). Retrieved from https://www.exim.gov/what-we-do/get-financing.

Loans. (n.d.). Retrieved from https://www.sba.gov/funding-programs/loans.

What We Do. (n.d.). Retrieved from https://www.wusata.org/whatwedo/overview/.

PART 5

The International Bank

CHAPTER 10

International Commercial Banking

Most small commercial banks have limited their scope to local business in the community. As more and more business has gone global, so have commercial banks. Today, almost all major banks have offices in major cities globally. Some banks have formed collaborations with other banks in foreign countries to better serve their trade partners. Because commercial banks make possible a reliable transfer of funds between different countries, they play an important part in financing international trade. In addition, international banks also serve as an indicator of the global economy's health and business trends.

The Structure of Foreign Banking Activities

Once a bank has made the decision to establish an overseas operation, there are a variety of organizational structures possible. The reason for this variety is due to such factors ranging from tax considerations to the bank's internal resources. The following list includes the most common structures found in foreign banking activities:

Correspondent Banking. Correspondent banks are banks that act as an agent on behalf of another bank, usually in another country. A correspondent bank performs many services such as managing foreign exchange, overseeing international investments, and facilitating transactions between exporters and importers. When a correspondent banking relationship is formed by two banks it is usually because one of them is not financially able to establish a branch in that country. By creating this relationship, the banks can retain customers while keeping costs down. The account that a correspondent bank maintains on behalf of foreign bank is referred to by the correspondent bank as *vostro*, meaning "your account (the foreign bank) on our books." This same account is referred to as the *nostro* account by the foreign bank meaning "our account on your (correspondent bank) books."

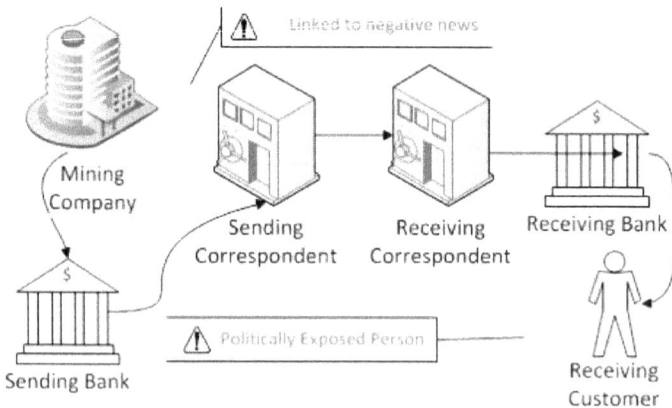

Figure 10.1 Correspondent Banking

Since so many international wire transfers occur between banks that do not have established relationships, a correspondent bank is required to be the intermediary. Wire transfers are often conducted through the Society for Worldwide Interbank Financial Telecommunication network (SWIFT). Using SWIFT to search for a correspondent bank, an originating bank may find a bank in which both create an agreement. The transferred funds are sent by the originating bank to the account held by the correspondent bank. The correspondent bank first collects its transfer fee from the customer then sends the money to the receiving bank. The standard fee for this transfer can be anywhere from $25 to $75.

Representative Office. While correspondent banks provide important sources of referrals for international trade, they sacrifice a great deal of potential income when they provide services through a correspondent rather than through their own operations. Many international banks remedy this problem by creating a representative office in which the bank establishes a physical presence in the foreign market but with very limited functions. A representative office cannot provide traditional banking services. It essentially serves as a marketing function for the parent bank which is not located in the host country. Consequently, representative offices provide minimum services to exporters and importers.

Branch Office. A branch office of a parent bank usually provides more legal functions. In practice, foreign bank branches are often independent, making most decisions locally. Branches may perform all banking functions permitted by the host country, including accepting deposits and extending loans. The predominant activity of a branch office is to extend credit.

Consortium Banks. Foreign banks may join forces to enter new markets, reducing the capital requirements and risks involved. Consortium banks are nothing more than a group of banks forming a joint venture to enter a new market. Recently, this business model has fallen into disfavor, although consortium banks remain a possibility for foreign trade.

The Scope of Foreign Banking Activities

Foreign banking has grown exponentially since the 1960's. Much of the international banking activity is focused in London where the financial skills involved in foreign trade have been acquired through years of experience. During the same time period, foreign banks have swarmed the U.S. market. The U.S banking authorities will allow international banks to compete with domestic banks. Because most international banks in the U.S. operate at the wholesale level, they are fairly difficult for the average exporter to locate.

Functions of International Commercial Banks

Credit Services

The primary function of the international commercial bank is to set up checking accounts in the form of deposits and to create loans. Lending is the major activity of the global commercial bank. The banks in overseas markets lend money to local importers or exporters in local currency. For example, Deutsche Bank's branch in Buenos Aires may lend pesos to a local manufacturer funded by peso deposits at its local branch. This type of lending is strictly local and competes with Argentine banks or other foreign bank branches.

The other form of lending, known as cross-border lending, involves a loan made to a borrower in a country other than the lender's local country. It is denominated in a currency other than that of the borrower. For example, Deutsche Bank's branch in Paris may loan U.S. dollars to the same manufacturer in Buenos Aires. The loan is made using dollars generated worldwide. Cross-border lending often takes the form of a syndicated or group facility.

Syndicated Loan Facilities

Syndicated loans are a major tool for international banks. These loans are widely used by banks to meet the needs of importers and exporters who want large scale and high-risk loans. A syndicated loan spreads the risk to a group of banks, usually on common terms. In this way, the risk which might be too large for one bank to accept on its own is spread out among the group of banks. It also helps to extend credit that would be too large for one bank to handle.

Trade Finance

The major activity of international banking is trade finance. The primary instrument of trade finance is the letter of credit which allows the credit of the bank to be substituted for that of the importer. This type of financing facilitates international trade between an exporter and an importer who otherwise would not be willing to trust the shipment of goods without some guarantee of advanced payment.

References

Correspondent Bank Definition. (n.d.). Retrieved from https://www.bankrate.com/glossary/c/correspondent-bank/

Duff, V. (2017, November 21). Role of Commercial Banks in International Business. Retrieved from https://smallbusiness.chron.com/role-commercial-banks-international-business-733.html

PART 6

Logistics and Insurance

CHAPTER 11

International Logistics

International logistics involves a chain of events. It starts at the purchase of the import and delivered to the exporter's warehouse, from there moving form there through delivery to the port of origin, loading the products on the ship, transporting the product from the port of origin to the port of destination, passing through the port of destination and customs imposed by the local country, exiting from the port of destination, and finally transporting to the importer's warehouse.

Categories of Logistics

Business logistics, according to Seyoum (2014), may be divided into two categories:

1. Materials management, for the most part, deals with product entering a country. This means the timely movement of product from the supplier to the manufacturer as inbound materials. This may also include the purchase of raw materials, transit, inventory management, and the distribution process. For

example, products can be assembled in Canada for distribution in Canada and the United States (Seyoum,p109).

2. Physical distribution, unlike materials management involves the outbound movement of an exporter's product to the ultimate buyer. It may include outbound transportation, inventory management and the proper packaging of the export product to reduce damage during shipment.

The Importance of International Logistics

There are at least three reasons that make international logistics important:

1. International logistics contributes to the efficient allocation of scarce resources globally. It allows countries to export products in which they have a comparative advantage, that is, the products that they make most efficiently. It also allows importing products that are either too costly in their own country to manufacture and/or are produced at a more competitive price in another country.

2. International logistics also contributes to economic growth. As exporters and importers expand their ability to procure and distribute raw materials and finished products, they expand the economy of other countries with respect to more competitive businesses, more employment opportunities, and a higher standard of living.

3. Advanced logistics systems increase the efficiency of production, transportation, and distribution of international trade. Seyoum (2014) cites the pharmaceutical and healthcare companies that have reduced costs associated with inventory, overhead, labor, and warehousing, but at the same time, outsourcing logistics to third-party operators. In addition, when various transportation modes are applied in the advanced distribution process, it

reduces the need for additional inventory. Finally, distribution is facilitated through shipment consolidation for large shipments without impacting the length of the journey.

The International Logistics Process

In the export-import transaction, the following steps represent the timeline of physical movement and distribution of exports from the exporter to the importer.

Step 1. After negotiations between the exporter and importer are finalized, the importer will place a purchase order to obtain the desired exports. In this purchase order, the importer will include terms of sale, payment method, and other conditions. It is assumed both the exporter and importer have made efforts to ensure there are no government restrictions on the merchandise in question. When the exporter receives the importer's purchase order, he will confirm receipt of the order and give the commitment to fulfill the order based on the given terms and conditions. At this point, the trade contract is final and creates a binding obligation. The exporter's proforma invoice is prepared which outlines the essential terms and conditions of the sale. If there is no production involved by the exporter, the prospective exporter must still meet packaging, labelling, and other documentary requirements. The exporter prepares the order for shipment which is then picked up by the importer's transit company according to the appropriate incoterm.

If the exporter must manufacture the product, the terms of the sale become the directions for production. At this point, the exporter is at risk that the importer may cancel the transaction leaving the exporter with the unfinished goods and costs incurred in production. Otherwise, at the end of the production process, the exporter prepares the order for shipment.

Step 2. Most often, small exporters and importers will use the services of a freight forwarder who will arrange for the exported goods to be picked up and delivered to the port of origin. Usually, the freight forwarder will select the mode of transportation, i.e. by air, ocean freight, rail, or by truck. Any one of these companies will book the necessary space for the cargo. The forwarder will confirm booking the cargo with the exporter, who in turn will confirm with the overseas importer.

Step 3. The shipping company will load the cargo at the port of origin where the merchandise will be transported to the importer. If pre-shipment inspection is involved, the cost is usually the responsibility of the importer. Pre-shipment inspection assures the importer that the shipment conforms to the sales contract. After the merchandise is loaded and transported, the freight forwarder sends to the customs broker the necessary documentation. The function of the customs broker is to clear the exports for the overseas importer at the port of destination. The customs broker submits documents in behalf of the overseas importer to the overseas customs to obtain release of the product. In many countries, tariffs and duties must be paid before this release. Also, customs agents may physically examine the shipment. At this point, penalties may be imposed for serious errors for problems found in the documentation. The customs broker notifies the forwarder when the merchandise is released.

Step 4. In this step, the carrier transports the merchandise from the port of origin to the port of destination. The most often used carrier at this step is the ocean freight company. It is the least expensive but most time-consuming method of transit. Most often, air carriers will offer the fastest delivery but at the most expensive cost. Since most trade today is intermodal, the carrier may be a combination of trucking, ocean freight, rail, and air transport companies.

Step 5. At this point, the cargo is unloaded at the port of destination, the point of entry. The customs services will inspect the documentation for any irregularities. If there are none, customs will clear the shipment provided all tariffs and duties are paid.

Step 6. The merchandise, once released by customs, will be picked up by the importer's transit company and transported to their warehouse.

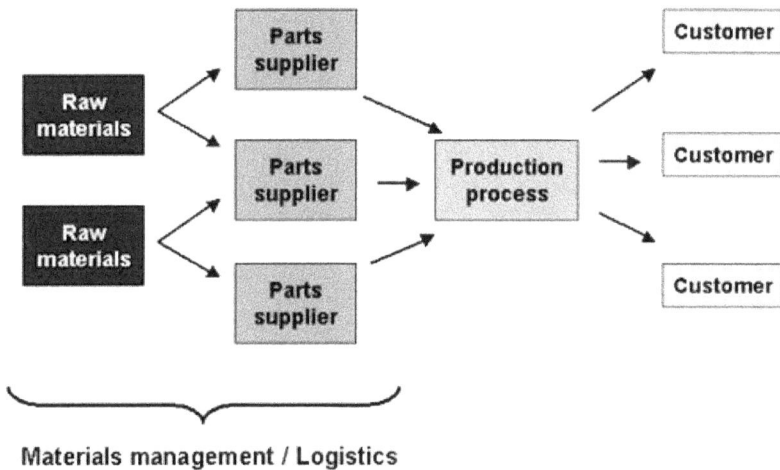

Figure 11.1 The Logistics Process

Logistics Risk

In the export-import process, international finance divides the logistics process and the order of physical movement into three classes of risk. Each class has a variety of financing methods. The classes are as follows:

| PRE-SHIPMENT RISK | SHIPMENT RISK | POST-SHIPMENT RISK |

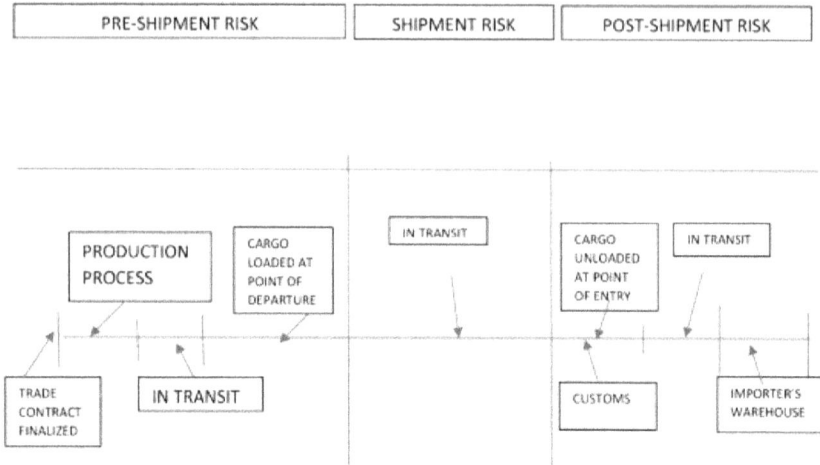

Figure 11.2 The Trade Cycle and Logistics Risk

Types of Logistics Risk

PRE-SHIPMENT RISK

Pre-shipment risk is the class of logistics risk that involves the finalizing of the contract between the exporter and importer. It may include the production process of manufacturing (if necessary) along with packaging, labeling, and other documentary requirements. Arrangements are made for transit of the final product from the exporter's warehouse to the port. Once inside the port the cargo is loaded onto the ship at the point of departure. As a result of correspondence between the exporter and importer, the importer opens a purchase order in behalf of the exporter to invoice the purchase of the desired merchandise and final payment by the importer. During this class of risk, a variety of events may occur to disrupt the transaction which include cancellation of the order by the importer, accidents in transit to the port, and failure to meet the deadline for the ship's departure. During the pre-shipment phase of the transaction, a freight forwarder usually arranges for the pickup and delivery to the port. They will also choose the mode of transit (rail, air, ocean) as well as reserve the necessary space for the cargo on the ship.

SHIPMENT RISK

Once the cargo is loaded on board the ship, the transaction enters the shipment risk phase. During this phase, the major risks involved include damage to the cargo container such as running aground by the ship, ramming by another ship, and jettison of the cargo when a general average is declared. General average is a marine insurance term that will be defined in the following chapter on insurance.

POST-SHIPMENT RISK

Post-shipment risk is a class a risk that begins at the arrival of the merchandise at the port of destination, clearing the goods through the customs office, and transit to the importer's warehouse. After the merchandise is transported, the freight forwarder sends the necessary documents, namely, the commercial invoice, the customs invoice, the packing list, the bill of lading, and certificate of origin (if necessary) to the customs broker who will clear the merchandise for the importer at the port of destination. The freight forwarder then arranges for pickup of the importer's merchandise from customs and arranges for transit to make delivery to the importer's warehouse. During this phase, the major risks encountered include trouble with customs requirements and accidents in transit to the importer's warehouse.

References

Erb, C., Campbell, H., & Tadas, V. (1996, November). Political Risk, Economic Risk and Financial Risk. Retrieved from http://people.duke.edu/~charvey/Country_risk/pol/pol.htm.

CHAPTER 12

Insurance

Risks in Foreign Trade

When export/import trade is conducted, companies face a number of risks that may adversely affect their operations, exposing them to losses. The risks of loss include political actions such as wars, revolutions, terrorist attacks and labor strikes that disrupt the internet. In addition to political actions, exporters face credit risks such as delays or loss of payment from importers. A third type of risk would include loss/damage to the exporter's shipment during transit.

Risk Insurance

Risk insurance exists to mitigate losses from all three categories mentioned in the previous paragraph. For political risk and credit risk the EXIM Bank offers insurance policies to cover the exporter. For loss of product, marine insurance exists to compensate those who are impacted by the losses.

Political Risk

The definition of political risk is the risk that a government may impose restrictions on trade or payment for trade to the exporter. In addition, a government may limit or control the exports and imports from and into its boundaries, known as embargoes. They may also restrict licenses to trade with foreign countries and impose currency controls.

Monitoring Political Risks

To keep informed of the likelihood of political unrest there exists third-party firms that offer monitoring services. In fact, specialized sources exist for specific countries that provide political risk services. Government agencies such as the U.S. Department of State, the Central Intelligence Agency of the United States, and the Export-Import Bank of the United States provide country risk reports. The U.S. Department of Commerce and its subdivision, known as the U.S. Commercial Service, provides the widest range of country reports that detail the advantages and disadvantages of doing business in a country along with its political risk.

Insuring Against Political Risks

When doing business internationally, the Export-Import Bank of the U.S. covers liability for both commercial and political risks. The EXIM Bank's multi-buyer credit insurance is a policy designed to protect the exporter's accounts receivable from non-payment. Given the protection of the policy, it equips businesses with the confidence necessary to enter new and unknown markets. Exporters may use the insurance to do the following:

- Extend credit terms to foreign customers
- Insure against nonpayment by importers

- Cover political risk
- Arrange financing through a lender by using insured receivables as additional collateral

Benefits of Credit Insurance

One of the major benefits of multi-buyer credit insurance is the reduction in risks it achieves. This risk reduction can safeguard against catastrophic losses when the importer does not pay. The EXIM Bank's coverage includes 95% exporter's sales invoices. In addition, credit insurance makes the exporter more competitive because it unlocks the ability to offer buyers the credit terms they require to do business with the exporter. Finally, the insurance provides credit management expertise. By leveraging the EXIM's international expertise, it eases the burden of credit risk management by the exporter.

How Credit Risk Insurance Works

The risk insurance policies from the EXIM Bank cover both commercial (credit) and political losses at 95%. There are no application fees or minimum premium payment. To issue the policy, the EXIM Bank requires a one-time refundable advance deposit of $500. The exporter's premium payment is paid no later than 30 days after the month of shipment. To qualify, two years of financial history must be provided.

Marine Insurance

Risk Mitigation

A type of insurance designed to cover the risk to the damage of the contents involved with the transportation of foreign trade by land, sea, rail, or air is known as marine insurance. It also covers damage to the ship belonging to the transportation company and to the liability for 3rd parties arising out of the process.

Marine insurance covers the liability of loss of the trade merchandise between the points of origin and the final destination regardless of the mode of transit. In addition, it covers losses connected with any transport by which the merchandise is transferred, acquired or held between the points of origin and the final destination.

Cargo Loss

There are two terms used to distinguish the degree of proof that a cargo has been lost or damaged. The first term, actual total loss, occurs when the losses from damages or the cost of repair equal or exceed the value of the property. The second term, constructive total loss, is a situation where the costs of repairs plus the cost of salvage equal or exceed the value of the property. Salvage may be performed by third parties such as tugboat companies. Since marine losses include losses of ships at sea, marine insurance differs from non-marine insurance in how the insured is required to prove their loss.

Extent of Cargo Coverage

As in any other insurance policy, marine insurance policies list the extent of coverage provided. The levels of cargo coverage fall into two categories: the first category is known as with average (WA), which covers less than as well as total losses. The second category, known as free of particular average (FPA), covers only total losses.

1. **With average coverage** – This type of policy indemnifies against partial losses by perils of the sea with the condition that the damages or losses amounts to 3% or more of the value of

the shipment. If the standard indemnifications exist, the 3% requirement is waived and losses are indemnified in full. Perils of the sea include ramming, running aground, sinking, fires, and jettison.

2. **Free of particular average** – "Free of" particular average followed by other words or phrases mean that the insurer assumes no responsibility for whatever is enumerated. If a policy reads "free of particular average" the insurer will not pay any particular average claim. Since the insured must therefore assume the risk for any and all partial losses, this is the most restrictive qualification on a marine insurance policy.

General Average – A Loss Mitigation Convention

Most of the marine insurance industry's practices related to proving the insured's losses can be traced back many centuries. Although attempts have been made to modernize the industry's terminology, several traditional expressions still exist. The rights and duties of both the insurer and the insured are clear and unambiguous. Two types of losses exist based on the term "average". The term "average" refers to allocation among all interested parties of a loss. They are general average and particular average. As used in the marine insurance industry, the word average has nothing to do with the normally accepted mathematical meaning. A particular average means a partial loss. General average means the owners and other shippers on board the ship proportionately are liable and contribute to fully reimburse those who have sustained a loss.

General Average

As started earlier, the term "average" refers to allocation among all interested parties of a loss. In order for general average to be declared, three conditions must exists. The first condition is that the event must be beyond the ship owner's control that imperils the entire shipment. Second, one of the shipper's (exporters) must have agreed to make a voluntary sacrifice. Third, in order for this sacrifice to be successful, there must be something saved such as the shipment at risk. With respect to voluntary sacrifice, they may include the jettison of certain cargo and the use of tugs.

The majority of general average claims are usually attributed to sinking, onboard fires, engine failures, mechanical breakdown of the ship. In the case of a general average, the captain of the ship orders the voluntary sacrifice of part of the cargo such as the number of containers it may take to lighten a ship that may sinking due to a tropical rain storm overwhelming its ability to drain the excess water. All the shippers who have containers on board are required to make a proportional contribution to cover the cost to reimburse for the jettison. Thus, any shippers, even if their containers were not jettisoned, may have a general average claim levied against them.

Partial Average

A particular average is a partial loss that is incurred by the shipper whose containers or merchandise are jettisoned. When there is a particular average loss, other shippers whose goods were not damaged do not contribute to the partial recovery of the shipper whose containers were jettisoned. An example of a particular average or partial loss may occur when a fire or storm damage is limited to a shipper's cargo and no other shipper has to sacrifice their container to save the ship. The container owner whose goods were damaged will refer the loss to their insurance company for indemnification, provided the policy covers the specific loss incurred. Most losses incurred by shippers are partial averages or losses.

Types of Policies

There are two types of marine insurance policies, the perils-only policy and the all-risks policy.

1. Perils-only policy

The perils- only policy covers the liability for extraordinary and unusual perils not expected during the voyage. Policy indemnifies the policyholder for loss or damage to the cargo or container caused by such events as onboard fires, explosions, sinking, running aground, ramming by another vessel, and jettison (general average sacrifice). Excluded items include pilferage or the unseaworthiness of the cargo ship.

2. All-risk policy

This policy offers the broadest coverage in marine insurance. The policyholder is indemnified against all perils of the sea but not to include damages from the risk of war, strikes, and civil strife. Additional coverage may be purchased to cover these exclusions. Additional coverage is usually provided through an endorsement on the existing policy.

References

General Average Vs. Particular Average. (2015, April 8). Retrieved from http://ghanashippingguide.com/2015/04/general-average-versus-particular-average-loss/.

Kantharia, R., Rajaratnam, A., Ganesan, S., Bruno, N., John, K., Drew, A. Agarwal, A. (2019, October 2). Different Types of Marine Insurance & Marine Insurance Policies. Retrieved from https://www.marineinsight.com/maritime-law/different-types-of-marine-insurance-marine-insurance-policies.

GLOSSARY

Air Waybill – provides detailed information about an air shipment and allows it to be tracked.

ASEAN – (Association of Southeast Asian Nations) economic agreement made to remove trade barriers in the emerging countries in Southeast Asia. Members: Indonesia, Thailand, Singapore, Philippines, Malaysia, Vietnam, Brunei, Cambodia, Myanmar (Burma), Laos.

Bill of Exchange – a promissory note written by one party that obligates a second party to pay a certain sum of money to the drawer.

Bill of Lading – Of the shipping documents, it is the most important because it provides detailed information for ocean shipments. It acts as a contract between the transportation company and the exporter, and acts as the title of ownership that establishes control over the shipment.

Business Norms – a culture's set of rules for conducting business

Certificate of Origin – document that qualifies exports for preferential duty treatment. Used most often by the World Trade Association members and in free trade areas such as NAFTA.

Common Market – a group of countries imposing few or no duties on trade with one another and a common tariff on trade with other countries. For example, a name for the European Economic Community or European Union, used especially in the 1960s and 1970s.

Consular Invoice – an invoice, which varies in its details and information requirements from nation to nation, that is presented to the local consulate in exchange for a visa to conduct trade.

Corporation – a legal entity that can engage in all functions of a business, such as entering contracts and lawsuits while being subject to a different tax rate

Culture – the customs, arts, social institutions, and achievements of a particular nation, people, or other social group.

Customs Union – a group of countries that have agreed to charge the same import duties as each other and usually to allow free trade between themselves.

Commercial Invoice – A document that contains an authoritative description of the merchandise shipped, including full details on quality, grades, price per unit, and total value, along with other information on terms of the shipment.

Competitive Pricing – a pricing approach that establishes export prices by maintaining the same price level as the competition, reducing prices or increasing the price with some level of product improvement.

Cost-based pricing – the most common pricing approach used by exporters that is based on full-cost-oriented pricing. Under this procedure, a markup rate on full cost is determined and then added to the product's cost to establish the price.

Demand-based Pricing – Using this approach, export prices are based on what consumers are willing to pay for the product or service. Market surveys will help supply the data to identify the level of demand.

Destination Control Statement – clause on certain documents that states that the item can only be exported to specified destinations.

Direct Exporting – exporting that is done between an exporter and importer, with no third party involved.

Dock Receipt – transfers title of the shipment when it arrives at the home port and left with the international carrier for export.

Economic Union – economic integration that requires members to unify monetary and fiscal policy of member states

Effectively Connected Income – income from foreign sources, earned in a permanent establishment in the U.S.

Efficiently Connected Income – income earned by a non-resident alien of U.S. branch of a foreign company.

Embargoes – official ban on trade with a specific country.

Equilibrium Exchange Rate – exchange rate where the quantity of a supplied currency equals the quantity demanded at a certain exchange rate.

European Union – the world's most significant example of economic integration. Economic union made up of 28 countries on the European continent

Exchange Controls – legal restriction by a nation's government on currency transferred between countries.

Export Packing List – A list that itemizes the material in each individual package and indicates the type of package (e.g. box, carton). It shows weights and measurements for each package, and it is used by customs agents to check the cargo.

EXIM – (The Export-Import Bank) Bank created for the purpose of facilitating U.S. exports. Provides financing and credit insurance for small business.

Free Trade Area – agreement that removes trade barriers between members, and each participating nation sets its own policy for nonmembers

Foreign Capital Controls – government controls that restrict the flow of foreign capital in and out of the country

GATT – The General Agreement on Trade and Tariffs that was the precursor to the World Trade Organization (WTO). Established rules to promote free trade and settle disputes across the globe.

High-context culture – a culture that relies on implicit and nonverbal communications.

Importing – the process of bringing foreign goods into the domestic market.

Indirect Exporting – exporting is managed by a third-party company that assumes the risks and costs of international trade

Incoterms – are a set of rules which define the responsibilities of sellers and buyers for the delivery of goods under sales contracts. They are published by the International Chamber of Commerce (ICC) and are widely used in commercial transactions.

Insurance Certificate – An insurance company may issue a policy or a certificate. If the company issues a policy, an application must be completed by the insured for each shipment it makes and is very time consuming. An insurance certificate provides the insured with blank certificates that it completes with details of the goods, destination, type and amount of insurance required, etc. The complete certificates are mailed to the insurance company saving time and facilitating more efficient operations of international transactions.

Limited Liability Company (**LLC**)–is a corporate structure in the U.S. whereby the owners are not personally liable for the company's debts or other liabilities. They are hybrid entities that combine the characteristics of a corporation with those of a partnership or sole proprietorship.

Low-context culture – a culture that values individualism and relies on explicit communication.

Manifest – is a detailed summary of the total cargo of a vessel (by each loading port) for customs purposes. It covers condition of the cargo and summarizes heavy lifts and their locations.

Marginal Pricing – is a more common pricing approach in exporting. It is often used in businesses with underutilized capacity. In this approach, the price does not cover the product's total cost but instead includes only the additional cost to produce the product to be exported.

Monochronic culture – a culture that values punctuality and focusing on one task at a time.

Most favored nation – a country which has been granted the most favorable trading terms available by another country. A **most** favored **nation** **clause** (also called a **most** favored customer **clause** or **most** favored licensee **clause**) is a **contract provision** in which a seller (or licensor) agrees to give the buyer (or licensee) the best terms it makes available to any other buyer (or licensee).

NAFTA – The North American Free Trade Agreement (**NAFTA**) is an agreement among the United States, Canada and Mexico designed to remove tariff barriers between the three countries.

Partnerships – A legal form of business operation between two or more individuals who share management and profits. The two most common forms are general and limited **partnerships**.

Penetration-pricing policy – is based on charging lower prices for exports to stimulate market growth. Increasing market share and maximizing revenues may generate higher profits.

Political Risk – risk that may occur as a result of government actions that occur in the target country that jeopardize trade. Government actions include raising tariffs, creating embargoes, placing currency controls on all foreign transactions, and government confiscation of foreign assets.

Polychronic culture – culture that places less emphasis on the value of time, preferring, instead, to multitask and build relationships

Quotas – a government regulation specifying the quantity of particular products that can be imported to a country.

S-Corp – a corporate structure in which the earnings are taxed as individual income to prevent additional tax

Secured Loan – loan that is guaranteed by an asset. Banks will lend an amount equal to or close to the value of the asset.

Shipper's Export Declaration – is issued to control certain exports and to compile trade data. It is required for shipments valued at more than

$2,500. Carriers and exporters are also required to declare dangerous cargo with this document.

Skimming – charging a premium price in the export market. Skimming is used when there are few competitors and a unique product.

Sole Proprietorship – legal structure of business done under the name of a single owner without the formation of a separate entity.

Spot rate – the most recently displayed exchange rate that represents the latest transaction in the currency markets.

STRG (State Regional Trade Group) – representing different areas of the U.S., STRGs typically promote food exports by way of marketing and funding

Subsidies – government money granted to a specific industry to keep the price of a commodity at a specific level.

Tariffs – Taxes placed on specific imports. It can be used to raise revenue, to discourage purchase by local consumers of foreign products, or some combination of the two.

TRIPS – (Trade Related Aspects of Intellectual Property Rights) narrowed the way intellectual property rights are protected around the world by bringing them under common international rule

Unsecured Loan – loans granted by banks without collateral using only the borrower's signature as a guarantee of repayment.

WTO – (The World Trade Organization) international governing body that promotes free and fair trade in over 164 countries

APPENDIX A: INCOTERMS

Group E

Ex Works - Named Place

Ex Works represents the minimum obligation to the exporter. Under this term, the price quoted applies only at the point of origin and the seller agrees to place the exports at the disposal of the importer at the agreed place on the date or within the period fixed. Under this term, the seller must bear all costs and risks of the goods until such time as the buyer is obliged to take delivery thereof. The seller must render the buyer at the buyers request and expense assistance in obtaining the documents issued in the country of origin. On the other hand, the buyer must arrange for shipment from the manufacturer or warehouse, bearing all the costs and risks of bringing it to their desired destination. This means the buyer must take delivery of the goods as soon as they have been placed at the agreed place on the date or within the time fixed. Also, the buyer must pay export taxes, or other fees or charges due to exportation. The buyer must bear all costs and risks of the goods from the time they are obligated to take delivery.

Group F

FAS (Free Along Side)

The seller's responsibility is to place the goods alongside the vessel at the designated port on the date or within the fixed time period and pay any heavy lift charges where necessary up to this point. The seller must also provide a ship's receipt and be responsible for any loss or damage, or both, until the goods have been delivered alongside the vessel or on the dock. The buyer then bears all costs and risks for the goods from that point on, which means the buyer must give the seller adequate notice of the name, sailing date, loading berth, and delivery time to the vessel. The buyer must also arrange and pay for any storage charges on the wharf where necessary. He must pay and provide for insurance, ocean freight, and other transportation. For the seller's protection, he should provide in his contract of sale that marine insurance obtained by the buyer include standard warehouse to warehouse coverage.

Under FAS terms, the obligation to obtain ocean freight space and insurance rests with the buyer. Despite this obligation, in many transactions the seller obtains the freight space, the marine insurance, and provides for shipment on behalf of the buyer. Therefore, seller and buyer should have an understanding as the whether the buyer will obtain the ocean freight space and insurance, as is his obligation or whether the seller agrees to do this for the buyer.

FOB (Free on Board)

Under this term, the price quoted applies at an inland shipping point. The seller arranges for loading of the goods on, or in rail cars, trucks, aircraft, or other conveyance for transportation. The seller must place goods on conveyance for delivery to the inland carrier for loading. He must also provide a clean bill of lading, and be responsible for any loss or damage until goods have been placed in conveyance at the loading point and the clean bill of lading has been furnished by the carrier.

The buyer must be responsible to pay export taxes or other fees levied because of exportation. Also, the buyer must be responsible for any loss or damage, or both incurred at the name point of departure.

In relation to FOB terms, the following cautions are recommended: The method of transportation such as trucks, rail cars, barges or aircraft, should be specified. If there are any switching charges involved during the land transportation, it should be agreed in advance whether these charges are paid by the seller or the buyer. Under the FOB terms, the buyer must arrange ocean freight space and marine insurance. Despite this obligation, many times the seller will obtain ocean freight and insurance and provide for shipment on behalf of the buyer. Seller and buyer should have an understanding as to whether the buyer pays the ocean freight/insurance as is his obligation or whether the seller agrees to do this for the buyer. Again, for the seller's protection, he should provide in his contract of sale that his marine insurance includes standard warehouse-to-warehouse coverage.

Group C

CFR (Cost and Freight)

Under CFR, the seller will quote a price that includes transportation to the designated point of destination. The seller's quotation must provide and pay for transportation to the main point of destination and pay for export taxes, fees and other charges levied by exportation. In addition, the seller must obtain and dispatch in a timely manner to the buyer a clean bill of lading to the main point of destination. At the buyer's request and expense, the seller must provide certificates of origin, consular invoices, or any other documents issued in the country of origin for which the buyer may require for importing goods to his country.

The buyer should accept all the documents when presented and receive goods upon arrival. This includes handling and paying for all subsequent movement of the goods. He should pay all costs of landing, including and duties, taxes and other expenses at the named destination point. The buyer must provide and pay for insurance and be responsible for loss of or damage to goods from the time and place at which the exporter's obligations cease. It is the buyer who pays the costs of certificate of origin, consular invoices or any other documents issued in the country of origin required for the importation of goods in the country of destination.

CIF (Cost, Insurance, Freight)

Under CIF, the seller quotes a price that includes the costs of the goods, marine insurance, and all transportation charges to the named destination point. This requires a seller to provide and pay for transportation to the named point of destination, to pay export taxes and to provide and pay for marine insurance. The seller must also provide, at the buyer's request and expense, certificates of origin, consular invoices, and any other documents which the buyer may require to import goods into the country of destination.

The buyer must accept the shipping documents when presented and receive the goods upon arrival, pay for all subsequent movement of the goods, including delivery from the vessel that complies with the bill of lading clauses. The buyer pays all costs of landing, such as duties, taxes, and other expenses at the named point of destination. In the CIF quotation, the buyer pays for risk insurance provided by the seller and is responsible for loss of goods from which the seller's obligation has been excused.

Under CIF contracts the seller and buyer should be in complete agreement from the time the contract is finalized as to who is to pay in advance such as weighing or inspection charges. In addition, the quantity to be shipped on any one vessel, should be agreed upon in advance with a view to the buyer's capacity to take delivery upon arrival and discharge of the vessel, within the free time allowed at the port of importation. Since CIF terms are generally interpreted to provide that charges for documents are the responsibility of the buyer, in many of the transaction these charges are included in the quoted CIF price. Hence, both buyer and seller should agree in advance who is to pay these charges. The final point of destination must be known in the event the ship charges at a port different from the named destination.

In most cases, the seller is obligated to prepay the ocean freight but, in some cases, shipments are made and the amount of the freight and deducted from the invoice provided by the seller. In order to avoid misunderstanding, especially when foreign exchange fluctuations occur that might affect the actual cost of transportation, it is necessary to be in agreement upon this in advance. Therefore, the seller would always prepay the ocean freight unless there is a specific agreement with the buyer in advance that goods can be shipped freight collect.

Group D

DDP (Delivered Duty Paid)

Under this term, DDP means that the seller completes his obligation to deliver when the goods have been made available at the named place of destination in the country of importation. DDP is one of the incoterm rules widely used within international trade. The seller bears all the costs and risks involved in bringing the goods to the place of destination, including insurance and taxes. In addition, the seller has an obligation to clear the goods for export as well as import and to pay any duty for both and to carry out all customs formalities, irrespective of the mode of transportation selected. This term is usually used by a buyer who does not want to enter into any kind of transport contract and would rather let the seller handle these responsibilities right up to their door. In DDP shipping, the maximum obligation on the seller since it involves the delivery of the goods to the buyer at the agreed destination. In that sense, DDP should be considered as the opposite of Ex Works, which involves the buyer picking up the cargo from the seller's door.

One word of caution: Although it may appear that the importer has it easy, it may come at a cost. The reason is using DDP shipment, the buyer depends completely upon the seller for everything from the point of origin to the point of destination. It implies that the importer can be at be at the mercy of the exporter in terms of cost. It could be that lower costs could be procured by the buyer better than the seller. For example, an importer may have access to better rates and services in his country rather than the exporter who sits in another country and needs to use the services of a third party to do the work on their behalf.

APPENDIX B:
TRADE DOCUMENTS

Air Waybill

The air waybill is the most important document issued by air carrier and is non-negotiable. It covers the air transport of cargo from airport to airport. The airway bills have 11-digit numbers that can be used to make bookings and track the shipment. Most air waybills contain eight sets of different colors. The first three are originals. The first original is green in color and is the issuing carrier's copy. A second, colored pink, is the consignee's copy. The exporter is issued the third blue copy. The fourth copy, colored brown acts as the delivery receipt. The remaining four copies are white. This document accompanies the goods shipped by an international courier to provide detailed information about the shipment and allows it to be tracked. The air carrier issues the bill and the shipper uses it as a receipt. Multiple copies are required for each party involved to document it.

There are five main functions of an air waybill. First, the contract of carriage specifies the conditions of the air waybill for carriage documents. Second, the air waybill is evidence of the receipt of goods. When the exporter delivers goods to be forwarded, he receives the receipt, which is proof that the shipment was handed over in good condition. After completion, an original copy of the air waybill is given to the exporter as evidence that the goods have been accepted and as proof of contract of carriage. Third, the air waybill may be used as a freight bill which can be an invoice together with certain documents. It will indicated charges to be paid by the consignee, the agent, or the carrier. Fourth, an air waybill can serve as evidence that the carrier is in a position to insure the shipment and is requested to do so by the exporter. Finally, the airwaybill may serve as a customs declaration. It is proof of the amount of freight billed for the goods carried and may be needed for customs clearance.

Bill of Exchange (Draft)

A draft is an unconditional written order by one person to another, signed by the person giving it and requiring the person to whom it is addressed to pay either on demand (sight draft) or at a fixed future time (time draft) a certain sum of money to the bearer.

Most drafts involve three parties. The first party is the drawer who will issue, sign and send the draft to the second party, the drawee. The draft is addressed to the drawee and orders him or her either to pay or to accept when due the amount indicated on the draft. When the drawee accepts the draft, he or she offers to pay the certain amount. The third party is the payee who receives payment made by the drawee. Often, the payee and the drawer can be the same person. The payee may also be a third party or the bank at which the drawer has their account.

Bill of Lading (BOL)

The bill of lading is the most important of all shipping documents and it must be issued by the transportation company. The full name and address of the transportation company must appear on the bill of lading. The bill of lading is a title document. Usually the bill of lading is made out in the name of the exporter who may endorse it over to his or her bank that will finance the shipment. In this case, the bank retains title to the goods while they are being financed. Since the bill of lading acts as collateral, if the loan financing is not repaid to the bank it can use the BOL to claim the merchandise from the exporter. In this case the bank can sell the goods and liquidate the loan with the proceeds. The transportation company has no responsibility for the accuracy of the description of the goods in the BOL. Unlike the air waybill, a bill of lading deals with shipments via sea or land rather than air.

Ocean Bill of Lading

The most common form of BoL in international trade is known as the ocean bill of lading. It comes in many versions, there are two that are most common. The straight and the order bill of lading.

Straight (Non-Negotiable) Bill of Lading

Under the terms of the straight bill of lading, the shipment is consigned to a specific party. When the shipment arrives at the port of destination, the shipping company delivers the cargo to anyone who can prove they are the party named in the BOL.

This BOL is not required at the time of delivery of the goods because title cannot be transferred to any third party by endorsement or delivery of the BOL. The exporter and the bank lose control over the goods. Because of this fact, the straight BOL does not act as good collateral. It is rarely used where the exporter or the bank wish to retain title to the goods until they've been paid. On the other hand, the straight bill might be used for cash in advance, open account and consignment and the exporter is willing to lose control over the good because they have been paid already or because he or she trusts the importer completely.

Order (Negotiable) Bill of Lading

The order bill of lading makes is possible to be negotiable when it contains a phrase such as "consigned" to the order of (a named party). The consignee can transfer title by endorsement and delivery. Since ocean shipments are most often financed by a bank, most ocean bills are in negotiable form. The negotiable order BOL is usually made out to the order of the exporter who will endorse it in blank. This is the most preferred practice because banks can get bearer documents that they do not have to endorse themselves to pass title. Because order bills of lading represent goods in transit that are readily marketable and often fully insured, banks consider these documents to be good collateral. Generally the bank looks to the party being financed as the primary source of repayment.

Clean vs Foul of Bill of Lading

In the case of damage to import products or in poor conditions to that they might not survive the ocean voyage, these conditions are noted on the BOL causing it to be known as a foul bill. This notation limits the liability of the transportation company from subsequent damage claims by the importer when the goods are received. Foul bills of lading are not acceptable under the terms of a letter of credit. Exporters can get a clean bill substituted for a foul one when they replace the damaged products.

Through Bill of Lading

When an exporter must ship through a port to take delivery of the goods a through bill of lading can be useful. The through BOL is not an ocean BOL because it is usually issued by a railroad or trucking company. It contains all the information usually found in an ocean bill of lading and represents the transportation company's obligation to see to it that the goods get shipped from the inland port of origin to the inland port of destination. The carrier will arrange for payment to the ocean line at the point of departure.

Consular Invoice

Certain nations require a consular invoice for customs, statistical, and other purposes. To create a consular invoice, an exporter must obtain special blank forms obtainable at the foreign consular offices. Either the exporter or his or her forwarding agent can complete the form but they must use meticulous care in completing the forms, since even minor inaccuracies may delay customs clearance in the importing country. Worse still, it could involve the importer in heavy fines. After the exporter or freight forwarder has completed the consular forms, they are presented and sworn to at the foreign consulate located in the U.S. port of shipment. Most consular invoices require a fee to be paid to the importer's government.

Commercial Invoice

The main purpose of a commercial invoice is to serve as the official description of the goods shipped. It will contain complete details on quality, price per unit, and total price of the shipment as well as the shipping term such as FOB/CIF etc. The most important distinction between the bill of lading and the invoice is the payment terms. The CI will include the currency, place, method, and time of payment. Similar to the bill of lading, the commercial invoice will include both the names and addresses of both the exporter and importer, the number of packages, and any marks on them for customs purposes. The CI will also include a detailed explanation of other expenses that include transportation, insurance and fees collectible from the importer. Furthermore, the commercial invoice should name the vessel, the port of departure, and the port of destination.

While the commercial invoice usually involves the seller and buyer, additional 3rd parties may be included, such as banks and the importer's government. For example, some invoices have special requirements by the importer's government that they be translated into local languages or local measurements. Customs authorities insist on complete consistency between the different documents. This means the numbers and marks on the commercial and consular invoices, the insurance certificate and the bill of lading should agree exactly. Failure to comply often results in heavy fines for the importer or failure to allow importation of the goods. Consequently, it is extremely important for the exporter and the importer to know and comply with local requirements.

Certificate of Origin

This document enables certain countries to determine if the product qualifies for preferential duty treatment. It attests to the origin of the export product and is used in free trade areas such as NAFTA. For example, under NAFTA terms gives a more favorable tariff rate if the item is manufactured in the U.S. To qualify for the lower tariff rates, the importer must provide a certificate of U.S. origin.

Insurance Certificate

When a shipment is going overseas, marine insurance is purchased to protect against any loss or damage that may occur in transit. If the exporter insures the shipment, it is required to document the type of policy and the amount of coverage. Chapter 11 will cover insurance documentation in further detail,

Dock Receipt

The purpose of the dock receipt is to indicate the goods have been delivered to the dock of destination. It is a non-negotiable receipt issued by the transportation country. Generally, the receipt is forwarded to a railroad or trucking company who will deliver the goods to the importer. The dock receipt ultimately is delivered to the exporter. It contains full details on the shipment, including the name of the exporter, the vessel, port of destination, any customs numbers or marks on the packages, a general description of the goods, and their weight and cubic measurement. The dock receipt is also used to make up the bill of lading if there are notations on the receipt concerning damages, these are transferred to the BOL which them makes it a foul BOL.

Shipper's Export Declaration

Many governments attempt to compile export statistics. The U.S. government requires the completion of an export declaration on a Department of Commerce form. This document is issued to compile trade data and control the flow of certain exports. It is required for shipments valued over $2,500 and may include dangerous cargo. The completed form must be filed with U.S. customs authorities and information given on the form must accurately described the shipment.

Export Packing List

The packing list identifies the exact content of the individual packages exported, including their weight. The packing list is an addendum to commercial invoice and helps identify specific items by the importer and facilitates clearance through customs. Heavy fines for inaccuracies or misrepresentations may be levied by authorities in the importing country.

Manifest

A manifest is a detailed summary on the condition and location of cargo on a vessel, its passengers and crew for the use of customs and other officials. This document is generally created by the ships broker based on the contents of the BOL. The manifest is like a passport except it involves imported goods instead of passengers. The purpose of the manifest is to provide evidence as to the origin of the goods, the absence of contraband and property of belligerents not onboard the vessel.

ABOUT THE AUTHORS

Joseph Greco, Ph.D, is an international finance professor at the California State University at Fullerton. He brings real-time experience as a global trade consultant and CEO of Global Financial Strategies, an export-import company that has successfully conducted trade throughout the world. Dr. Greco has won many government grants to help promote trade and education between U.S. and foreign firms. With over 20 years of investment banking experience, he helped to raise capital to establish Metro Pacific Bank in Southern California. As an EXIM Bank broker, he holds licenses and certifications to train companies in offshore outsourcing. He has published articles and books on global finance, mainly covering emerging markets. Additionally, he has delivered many seminars, courses, and speeches on a wide variety of topics in international trade.

Brian Murray is a graduate of the California State University at Fullerton, where he majored in International Business with a concentration in Global Trade. During his academic career, he studied abroad at the SRH University in Heidelberg, Germany to complete a seminar in global strategic management. After graduation, he founded Crafted Trading to help independent U.S. breweries find export opportunities overseas. As a former student of Dr. Greco, he applied the practical knowledge of his startup experiences into the pages of this book.

www.ingramcontent.com/pod-product-compliance
Lightning Source LLC
Chambersburg PA
CBHW071648210326
41597CB00017B/2146